STEVE LONGENECKER'S

# Wilderness Emergency Medical Aid Book For Kids (& Their Adults)

almond, nc

Milestone Press, PO Box 158, Almond, NC 28702

Book design by Ron Roman/Treehouse Communications
www.treehousecomm.com

Illustrations by Frank Lee

**Library of Congress Cataloging-in-Publication Data**

Longenecker, Steve.
[Wilderness emergency medical aid book for kids & their adults]
Steve Longenecker's wilderness emergency medical aid book for
kids & their adults.
p. cm.
Includes bibliographical references.
ISBN 1-889596-18-3 (alk. paper)
1. Outdoor medical emergencies—Juvenile literature. 2. First aid in
illness and injury—Juvenile literature. I. Title.
RC88.9O95L66 2005
616.02'5—dc22
2005000202

Printed in the United States on recycled paper

Each individual is responsible for his or her own actions when choosing to assist in an emergency situation. This book is not intended as a substitute for first aid training. It is sold with the understanding that the author and publisher assume no responsibility for any adverse effects or consequences resulting from the teaching or use of any procedure listed or described herein. In any medical emergency, a trained professional should be consulted as soon as possible.

This book is dedicated
to everyone,
child or adult, who has ever benefited
or will benefit from
Wilderness Emergency Medical Aid.

# Acknowledgements

Many people have helped me with this undertaking, in many different ways.

First, my brother, Bill Longenecker, met Jim Parham of Milestone Press while biking in North Carolina and told him about my Wilderness Emergency Medical Aid programs for kids. Jim invited me to meet his wife and business partner, Mary Ellen Hammond. I'm grateful for their expertise and encouragement.

I'm also grateful to my friend Wayne Busch, RN, who wrote *The First Aid Kit* section.

In addition, I want to thank the following folks: Chris Abell, Donnie Bain, Rod Baird, Mark Bishop, Elizabeth Brown, Grant Bullard, Jamie Butler, Hope Byrd, Ginger Cecil, Matt Dahl, Brion Dixon, Steve Dixon, Robert Eshelman, Susan Frame, Maria Fysal, Robert John Gillespie, Jim Goodrum, Patti Gordon, Andrea Gravatt MD, Jim Kurrts, Brooks Lumpkin, Mike McCue, Chuck and Jean McGrady, Bob Miller, Brison Robertson MD, Steve Sandman, Christopher Stec, John Stovall, Gordon Swennes, Steve Walston, William Wallace, David Ward MD, Bob Watts, and Tricia Williams.

# Contents

1- Where's the accident?
2- What seems to be wrong?
3- How many people hurt?
4- What's being done for them?
5- Don't hang up!

**Appendix**

# Foreword

Each summer, hundreds of kids come to Falling Creek, a summer camp in western North Carolina. They spend their summer mountain biking, rock climbing, paddling, hiking, and participating in a wide range of sports. And at the end of each summer, to the surprise of their parents, many of them return home with a much better understanding of how to deal with life-threatening situations.

Why is that? Because Steve Longenecker has taught them how to respond to emergencies through his Wilderness Emergency Medical Aid (WEMA) classes. Kids know adults are there to protect them, but Steve poses two questions: What if the adult is the one who is hurt? And what if there is no adult around when a friend or relative is hurt?

These are easy ideas to understand at summer camp. Hiking trips and rock climbs are led by a camp counselor, but what if he is deathly allergic to bee stings or has an accident resulting in an injury? What if two campers are off mountain biking, and one of them takes a spill and is seriously hurt?

"What-if" questions are key components of WEMA training. What if you happen upon another kid who has cut himself and there's a lot of bleeding, what do you do? What if your uncle passes out while mowing the lawn, what do you do? What if you find a person unconscious and not breathing, what do you do?

WEMA teaches kids to think through what-if situations. Through role-playing, which most kids do really well, they learn how to deal with the unexpected and how to anticipate emergency situations. They also learn about prevention of accidents, since the goal is never to actually have to use the WEMA training.

Parents sometimes assume that we require kids to take WEMA classes. We don't. The kids voluntarily sign up, because the classes are fun, and because WEMA gives them the ability to save the life of a relative, a friend, or even someone they don't know.

For years, many of us have urged Steve to share what he has learned from his experience as a camp counselor, rock climber, and outfitter guide. As he relates in this book, his life was saved by the quick action of two friends whom he had taught how to respond in an emergency.

Each summer, we learn over and over again that a kid who has been properly trained has the ability to make a difference in an emergency situation. Sometimes years after leaving Falling Creek, a former camper will return, now an adult, to tell us how he responded to an emergency situation based on his WEMA training—how he made a difference.

This book is about teaching kids how to make a difference.

Chuck McGrady
January 1, 2005

*Chuck McGrady is owner and a director of Falling Creek Camp for Boys in Tuxedo, NC; a past director of the American Camping Association; and a director and past National President of the Sierra Club. Steve Longenecker was McGrady's camp counselor at Camp Sequoyah in 1968.*

# Prologue

## the story...

At first, the newspapers said I fell 88 ft. from the cliff and landed at my two friends' feet. Later, somebody measured the fall and found it was only 67 ft. At the time numbers didn't matter because my friends were sure I was dead, especially after they saw me bounce into the air as high as their heads, then fall back to the ground.

I made no movement, no sound, no nothing. They could tell from the blue-black color of my skin that I was not breathing—and they also knew that brain cells begin to die after about 5 minutes without oxygen.

This was not the way things were supposed to happen. I was the First Aid instructor, the rescue squad member, the enthusiastic volunteer in the emergency room at the local hospital. I was the one to whom people turned with medical questions, or when somebody twisted an ankle in a high school soccer game. What are you supposed to do when the "emergency person" is the one who's hurt?

So there I was—unconscious, undoubtedly injured, not breathing, and dying by the second. My personal "countdown to death" was under way.

Suddenly, my friends noticed the strap of my climbing helmet was shutting off my airway. Very carefully, because they were sure my neck was broken and they knew any movement could kill or paralyze me, they cut through the strap with a pocketknife. Suddenly, I began to breathe again.

My two climbing friends had learned their emergency procedures from me, never dreaming they'd be using them on their own teacher. Talk about a role reversal!

## ...the rest of the story

Because of what I had taught my two friends about how to respond in an emergency, and because of the way they used what they learned from me, I'm alive to tell this story.

Over the years following my climbing accident, I began to wonder why I had survived the fall in the first place. It occurred to me that perhaps the reason I lived to tell this tale was so I'd be around to teach others, specifically children and teenagers, how to respond when the adult in charge is hurt and unable to take charge. It was clear to me that this information could apply in all sorts of settings—not only in an outdoor adventure setting, like the one in which my life had been saved, but also at home, at school, or on a city street. Because to me, everyone has his or her own personal "wilderness," wherever events, surroundings, or both are unfamiliar and perhaps uncomfortable and frightening.

I developed a series of classes which I called Wilderness Emergency Medical Aid, or WEMA for short, and began teaching it to Scout, church, and school groups. At Falling Creek, the camp in North Carolina where I work as Director of Adventure Programs, we began holding workshops for counselors from other camps, so that they, too, could offer these skills to their campers. Over the years, many of my students have come back to tell me stories of how they put their WEMA skills to use in an emergency and made a difference, both to the injured person and to themselves. Teaching WEMA became some of the most satisfying work of my life.

I'm still teaching, and I don't intend to stop anytime soon. But I soon realized I'm getting older, and there is only one of me. How could I spread the information to more people?

The next step seemed obvious: I should write a book to help other adults teach the WEMA classes. But how to do that presented a real challenge. My primary means of communicating is talking, and in my line of work I do most of my talking to kids. Now I wanted to reach kids through their adult leaders and teachers. (I also know some kids are curious and motivated enough to want to read and learn about it on their own.)

That's how this book was born. It serves two purposes. First, it's a manual for adults, providing a curriculum, with teaching tips, for grown-ups—camp counselors, teachers, Scout and church leaders, and parents—who want the kids in their charge to be prepared to respond appropriately and helpfully in an emergency. Second, it's a resource text for kids themselves. Much of it is written the way I talk. Frank Lee's illustrations help get the message across in a visual manner.

## What This Book Won't Teach You

Although the Table of Contents gives you an idea of what's in this book, I want to be perfectly clear about what's *not* in it. You'll find information on how to set priorities in an emergency situation and *what* to do, but not necessarily *how* to do it. For example, you won't find detailed instructions for dressing a wound, splinting a broken bone, stabilizing a head and neck to prevent spinal damage, or performing CPR. There are plenty of resources for that information and training—your local hospital, Emergency Medical System (EMS), or the fire department.

In other words, I expect you to do that research and learning on your own, and if you want to be a good teacher or student, you'll have to. If you're an adult teaching a group, I suggest you call in specialty trainers to teach your kids those skills. If you're a kid reading this book on your own, sign up for a first aid class to get those skills. In this book, you'll find out how to use that "first aid kit in your head" to put all of the skills to use and make a positive difference in an emergency situation—maybe even save a life, the way my own life was saved back in 1972.

# Introduction

Two distinct groups of people will be reading and studying this book. One group will be mostly adults: parents, educators, group leaders, camp counselors. I hope they will all share one common goal: to *teach* this information to children and young adults. For this first group, I've written a long introduction that emphasizes the teaching of this material. The second group for whom this book is intended is made up of young people like the ones in the many youth groups I've worked with over the years. I hope this second group will want to *learn* the material presented in the book. A short, separate introductory section directed specifically to kids follows the introduction for adults.

## To the Teacher

What parents, teachers, coaches, Scout leaders, or camp counselors wouldn't want the children in their charge to know what to do if the grown-up was the one who needed help? (If you are a kid reading this book, surely you'd want to know what to do if your parent, Scout leader, or teacher got hurt.) Most people would want those around them, regardless of their age, ready and able to help if they were hurt.

This, of course, is a dramatic switch in traditional roles, when a physically traumatic event is witnessed by the child. In an instant, the adult in charge is in distress and needs the young person's assistance. Or, the injured person may be another child—a brother, sister, or best friend. For a young person in this position without knowledge of how to help, a serious accident is more than a terrifying experience; it could turn into a memory that haunts her for a lifetime.

Will the child know what to do if the injured person is not breathing? Bleeding severely? Unconscious, and unable to respond? Does he know how to call for professional assistance? If you are the victim, can he protect you from further injury by asking bystanders not to move you unless it's absolutely necessary to prevent complications?

This is a lot to expect a child to know, but teaching it could mean you've given her the tools to save your life and/or the lives of others. In this book, I've tried to couch relevant information in an engaging, readable form you can use to empower children within your sphere of influence.

After recovering from my climbing fall, I continued to take kids out on trips. *But,* I thought, *what if I'm hurt again, and these little children are the ones who must take care of me?*

I wanted everyone with me on a trip to know what to do in an emergency. Prior to my accident, I had always been the one who tended to any injuries or illnesses. It took my being seriously injured, and seeing my companions as potential rescuers, to start me thinking about "what if?" I began asking, *What if I were to cut my foot severely while chopping wood? Could you stop the bleeding? How about going for help? Who would go, and what would be taken along? Why?*

I wouldn't be at all surprised if there are children now in your life who consider you their hero. Whether you're a parent, teacher, pastor, rabbi, camp counselor, or a youth leader with another title, chances are you are admired by kids in your care.

After September 11, 2001, the definition of "hero" changed dramatically. Whereas before it might have meant an athlete, rock star, or TV personality, after that date many others were recognized for their courage under incredibly challenging circumstances when the World Trade Center was attacked.

As you begin teaching kids how they can help in a medical emergency, keep in mind you are preparing them to be heroes. Wouldn't it be amazing if one of those students became *your* hero?

## What is "WEMA"?

Wilderness Emergency Medical Aid (WEMA) is the name I gave to the classes I created and required children to take before they could go with me on backpacking or rock climbing outings at camp.

*Any child who finds herself in a situation where the supervising adult is critically injured, and where she, the child, must take charge, is most definitely going to be in a "wilderness."*

For a while, I insisted they be trained before taking these trips. These days I believe it's more important the kids be the ones making that decision. However, I feel much better when they *are* WEMA-trained—and for the record, so do they!

When I first conceived the name for this program, more than one person asked me about the word "Wilderness." After all, I was talking about carrying cell phones, calling 911, and other things not typically thought of as part of a wilderness experience.

My response was, and still is, that everyone has their own personal wilderness. It's a place that's unfamiliar and scary, where you're unlikely to feel uncomfortable. It can be in the middle of a city, deep in the woods, or up in an airplane. (In fact, you may feel you're entering a bit of a "wilderness" in thinking about teaching this subject!) Any child who finds herself in a situation where the supervising adult is critically injured, and where she, the child, must take charge, is most definitely going to be in a "wilderness." The purpose of this book is to help you prepare her to deal with that wilderness.

I'm calling on you to reach the kids in your life and motivate them to become functional and competent in an emergency situation. Sure, they can pick up quite a bit by reading through this book themselves. But for truly learning and retaining the skills, there's no substitute for working hands-on in a group with an adult leader, systematically choosing one or several topics to go over in a session. Creating realistic emergency simulations where kids have to take leadership roles is a critical part of teaching this material effectively.

My goal with this book is to inspire you, the adult leader, to use what I have done to develop your own classes for teaching basic emergency procedures to children. I've tried to provide examples of what has worked for me by using scenarios, techniques, and "what-ifs" throughout. As the leader, you'll be responsible for providing the environment and exercises to help your students learn what to do should someone require their assistance. My initial examples will get you started, but many good suggestions will come from your kids, I promise! Listen to your group, and use ideas that best suit its needs.

## Teaching WEMA

This book and the information it contains is my gift to the future. It's the sum of the experiences I've had teaching children how to help themselves and others in a medical emergency. It's certainly not an exhaustive emergency medical text. On the contrary, it's my attempt to simplify emergency medical procedures into packets of information that could "do the job" in a critical situation. If this book is used as both a catalyst for teaching and one of your source books, I'd be honored.

For details on medical procedures, there is excellent material available in libraries, bookstores, and on the Internet. All good teachers must be resourceful; I trust you'll find the factual information you need. Throughout this book you'll find places where it's a good idea to bring in a trainer or skills expert to demonstrate procedures for your group.

*The WEMA curriculum teaches children to use their eyes, their ears, and even their intuition to observe and ask themselves the right questions about emergency situations.*

Your job is to
**1** choose the material,
**2** present it in a way that will mean something to your students, and
**3** find ways for them to practice what they've learned so they'll be prepared to use it if necessary.

At this point, are you questioning whether or not teaching WEMA is something you should be doing? Perhaps this little quiz will help convince you it's a worthwhile endeavor.

# Teacher Quiz

- Are there children in my life?
- Could they help me if I were injured and couldn't take care of the problem myself?

Fairly simple answers, right? Read on...

- Am I capable of showing them how to determine if outside assistance is needed in a medical emergency? (*Recognizing the Big 3,* p.28.)
- Can I explain, demonstrate, and conduct a 911 practice session? (*Contacting 911* p. 66.)
- Do they know what to do if my finger were to be amputated by a slamming car door, or what to do if I crash into a tree while skiing and see a chunk of my tongue in the snow, right there by my skis? (*When Parts Come Loose,* p. 112.)

The questions have become a bit more involved, haven't they? By the time you've read this book thoroughly, you'll be able to successfully teach—or be able to locate someone who can help you teach—skills to help kids with any of the situations listed above.

## WEMA's Most Important Lesson

Details of how to treat allergies, seizures, snake bite, appendicitis, hypothermia, how to splint a broken bone, or immobilize someone with a potential spinal injury would make this book too cumbersome and defeat its purpose. My aim is to educate kids not about *how* to do these procedures, but about *when* to use them and *why*. The WEMA curriculum teaches children to use their eyes, their ears, and even their intuition to observe and ask themselves the right questions about emergency situations.

*Triage* is a word you hear a lot on TV medical dramas. In a hospital emergency room, it's also a place—probably the first place you'll visit if you ever wind up in an emergency room—where time is of the essence in assessing and treating an injury or illness. Triage is the process of setting priorities and making choices.

In WEMA, triage is the most important lesson you can teach. A medical emergency situation requires the constant making and modifying of choices. The material and exercises in this book are all about preparing children to make positive choices when that time comes. With this book, you can make a difference in children's lives, and maybe even your own, by helping prepare them.

*In WEMA, triage is the most important lesson you can teach. A medical emergency situation requires the constant making and modifying of choices.*

A good teacher takes a student to a certain point, then releases the student's hand and watches him walk forward into the future. My book now becomes your book. I wish you great rewards in teaching WEMA skills to the children in your charge.

# To You, the Kid

Did you ever want to see what was in the teacher's manual, the book that looked sort of like your textbook, but had all the answers in it? In a sense, you're looking at that book right now. It's designed to help you learn what to do if you find yourself in a situation where someone is hurt—perhaps badly hurt—and you happen to be the only one on the scene who knows what should and should not be done. This book is not just for adults, it's for everyone to read, including you. It has information on important things like what to say and do when you call 911, how to recognize if someone's not breathing, how to take charge of a difficult situation, even what to do if someone's finger comes off.

*You're a little bit afraid, you say? Concerned about seeing blood, bones sticking out of someone's skin, or smelling vomit, perhaps? All of that is possible in a medical emergency.*

You're a little bit afraid, you say? Concerned about seeing blood, bones sticking out of someone's skin, or smelling vomit, perhaps? All of that is possible in a medical emergency. However, your greatest concern

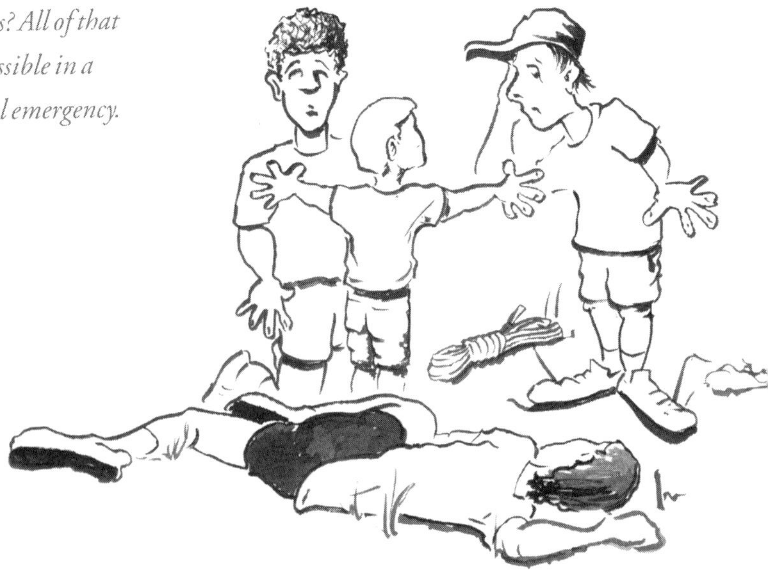

will likely be how to help the person who is hurt. You'll want to know what to do to keep things from getting worse. You'll want to know how to get medical help and make the person comfortable until medical help arrives. When the emergency is over, or when someone else has arrived to take charge of the situation, you may want to cry, scream, shiver, or just be alone in a quiet place. That reaction will be normal and natural; you will have done all you could do. In the event of an emergency when you may need to take charge, this book offers a way to prepare yourself.

Think about it—everyone who might need your help is going to be a stranger, a friend, or a member of your family. Take a moment to consider which one of those would be hardest to help in an emergency. Which one are you most likely to be helping? It is usually a family member or a close friend who needs help in a medical emergency. After all, you spend most of your time with family and close friends, right?

*We can't know the who or when or where of a medical emergency, but we can work on the what to do.*

We can't know the who or when or where of a medical emergency, but we *can* work on the *what* to do. This book has a lot of stories in it about kids in emergency situations. Some of them are true; some are made up. You'll read about emergencies in which kids just like you have to use their eyes and ears to assess a situation, make some important choices about what to do, and respond immediately. Sometimes they do the wrong thing or nothing at all, and the story doesn't end well. Sometimes they do exactly the right thing, like my friends did for me when I took the climbing fall described in the *Prologue*, and everything comes out just fine. There are even times when everything is done right, and the victim stays hurt or even dies.

The important thing is for you to learn the best action to take when you find yourself in a medical emergency. If you practice the skills you learn with a group, trust me—you'll know what to do when a real emergency happens.

# How This Book Works

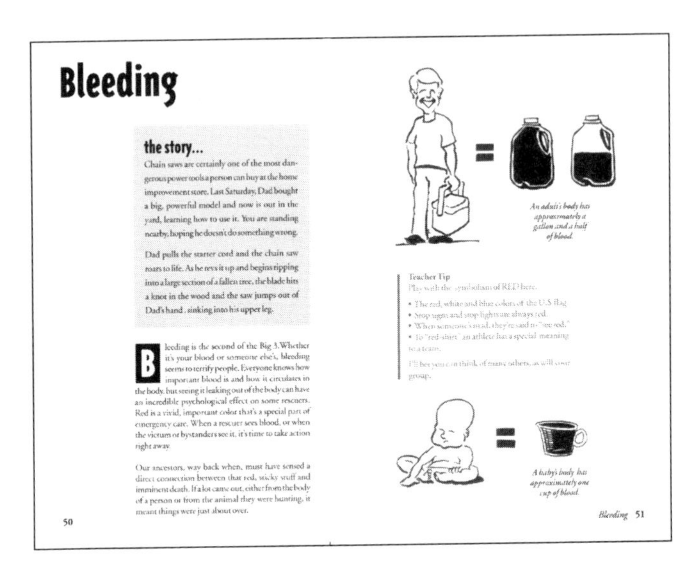

## Bleeding

**the story...**

Chain saws are certainly one of the most dangerous power tools a person can buy at the home improvement store. Last Saturday, Dad bought a big, powerful model and now is out in the yard, learning how to use it. You are standing nearby, hoping he doesn't do something wrong.

Dad pulls the starter cord and the chain saw roars to life. As he revs it up and begins ripping into a large section of a fallen tree, the blade hits a knot in the wood and the saw jumps out of Dad's hand, sinking into his upper leg.

Bleeding is the second of the Big 3. Whether it's your blood or someone else's, bleeding seems to terrify people. Everyone knows how important blood is and how it circulates in the body, but seeing it leaking out of the body can have an incredible psychological effect on some rescuers. Red is a vivid, important color that's a special part of emergency care. When a rescuer sees blood, or when the victim or bystanders see it, it's time to take action right away.

Our ancestors, way back when, must have sensed a direct connection between that red, sticky stuff and imminent death. If a lot came out, either from the body of a person or from the animal they were hunting, it meant things were just about over.

50

*An adult's body has approximately a gallon and a half of blood.*

Teacher Tip
Play with the symbolism of RED here.

- The red, white and blue colors of the U.S flag
- Stop signs and stop lights are always red.
- When someone's mad, they're said to "see red."
- To "red-shirt" an athlete has a special meaning to a team.

I'll bet you can think of many others, as will your group.

*A baby's body has approximately one cup of blood.*

*Bleeding* 51

he "meat" of the WEMA material is under *First Things First* and *Injuries, Etc.* In each of those chapters, you'll find specific sorts of information presented in different ways, both verbally and visually.

The heading of each chapter describes the type of problem we'll be dealing with. For instance, *Broken Bones* obviously deals with problems that arise when bones are fractured.

In most of the chapters, usually near the beginning, you'll find a story or scenario designed to get you thinking, "What would I do in a situation like this one?" It's clearly marked, *the story....* Be forewarned that the story will leave you hanging. Toward the end of the chapter you'll find its conclusion in *...the rest of the story.*

Also near the beginning of the chapter you'll find what could be called the "technical data" that relates to the topic. This is a brief explanation of what a rescuer will see, hear, or experience, and how the victim may respond in such a situation. The purpose of this information is to set the stage or to give guidelines so that anyone reading this book can put himself into the scene and then decide where and how he would proceed.

Sprinkled throughout the chapters you'll find teacher tips in various forms. These tips are directed to anyone using this book as an instructional manual while teaching a group of kids. Young folks reading on their own will find these tips informative as well, but they should realize these tips are intended to spark ideas in adults' heads, not as a way of checking to see if their instructor is teaching the material correctly.

Whenever I teach a WEMA class, I find my students provide me with an abundance of "what-if" questions. I've included a few in most sections as a painless way of sneaking in just a little more information about the subject. Also, for anyone using this text as a teaching aid, what-ifs are designed to enhance group interaction in role-playing scenarios.

Some chapters include sidebars containing important checklists, definitions, and other data. Sections in the *Appendix* contain information to enhance workshops and classes. *A Body of Facts* is simply interesting trivia that will add to a student's understanding of how the body works. The section on first aid kits begins with the idea that the best tools for emergency preparedness are in our heads and goes on to present basic facts on this subject. Finally, Frank Lee's illustrations underscore visually what I'm attempting to convey with words.

# First Things First

## Important Issues in Medical Emergencies

# Staying Safe

YOU
MUST
NOT
BECOME
A
VICTIM

he very first rule of emergency aid is for the rescuer to stay safe. Unfortunately, in the heat of the moment, it is often forgotten. It is imperative that no one else become a victim.

Until a rescuer can enter the scene of the emergency safely, it should not be entered at all. The first question a rescuer should ask is, "Is it safe to enter the scene?"

> **Teacher Tip**
> Scream it from the rooftops...
> smother it with "what-if" sessions...
> warn potential rescuers about it again and again...
>
> THE RESCUER MUST NOT BECOME A VICTIM!

Start with haste, stir-in a passionate desire to help, add lack of experience, and you have a recipe for serious trouble.

**If it is not safe to enter the scene, here is what you can do.**

- Find a phone and call 911 for EMS.
- Keep others from being hurt by encouraging them to move away from the scene.
- Warn others that this is a dangerous situation.
- Reassure them that professional help is on the way.

> **Teacher Tip**
> Whenever you have a what-if session, whenever you plan or debrief a simulation, whenever you put a question to your group about handling an emergency situation, make sure the very first thing they do is ask:
>
> "IS IT SAFE FOR ME TO HELP?"

Recognizing

# The Big 3

Not Breathing?
START IT!
severe BLeeding?
STOP IT!
Bumped head? unconcious?
IF Breathing, don't move the victim!!

I've been calling Breathing, Bleeding, and Bumped Heads the "Big 3" for so long now that I place special emphasis on them from the very beginning of my WEMA classes. They are covered in detail in separate chapters beginning on p. 42. Many injuries fall into one of these 3 basic categories, each of which requires specific initial assessments and simple but critical responses before anything else is done.

Responses to the Big 3 can be summed up succinctly:

- Not breathing? START IT.
- Severe bleeding? STOP IT.
- Bumped head? Unconcious? If the victim is breathing, permit absolutely no movement. Call for adult reinforcement and outside assistance immediately.

With the first two conditions (bleeding and breathing), haste is imperative; with the third (bumped heads), incredible care must be taken to prevent possible movement of the head, neck, or spinal column. In all cases of the Big 3, outside emergency assistance must be contacted as soon as possible.

**Learning for Life**

This is serious stuff for a child to absorb and learn. Are we asking children to recognize situations where inaction or improper action could have dire consequences? Yes. Are we teaching them skills that will be theirs for a lifetime, even though those skills may be used rarely, if ever? Yes.

Are we telling them that as long as they know what to do, there will always be a happy ending? No.

Are we suggesting to kids (and to ourselves) that they will be more caring and compassionate people when they've learned these skills? Most definitely!

Kindness and consideration are learned behaviors, best modeled for children by people they admire. I firmly believe kids would rather help than hurt, and be of use in an emergency than be the cause of it. A wonderful benefit of WEMA training is that it empowers children to be helpful and useful—in emergencies, but also in the less challenging situations of everyday life.

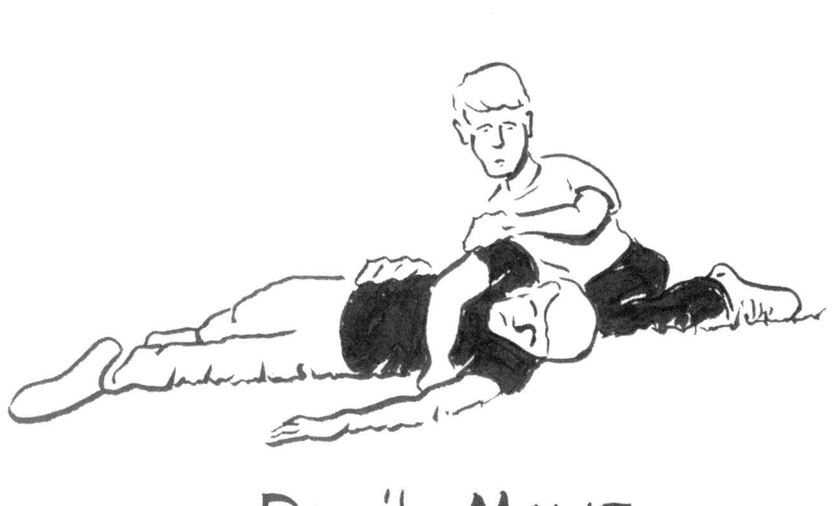

DON'T MOVE THE VICTIM!!

**Teacher Tip**

I strongly encourage you to develop your own personal way of organizing and presenting this information. Don't like the "Big 3" idea as a mnemonic device? Try the checklist below as a way to remember the first steps in assessing an emergency situation.

Yet another mneumonic is T IA. To medical personnel, TIA stands for *transient ischemic attack,* meaning "little stroke." But let's co-opt it here to mean "Time for Initial Assessment."

However you remember these important initial assessment steps, make sure you stress their importance when a rescue makes first contact with a victim. Once these steps have been taken and EMS is on the way, sometimes all that can be done is to render "little c.p.r." (covered next, beginning on p. 32).

**Rescuer's Checklist**

- Take a deep breath, maybe even whisper a prayer.
- Say to yourself, "I can help!"
- Is it safe to enter the scene?
- Start with "A, B, C, C!" (see p. 30)
- Is the injury life-threatening or not?
- Do I need outside help?

# Notes:

# little c.p.r.

CPR = Cardiopulmonary Resuscitation

little cpr = comfort protection reassurance

In many emergency situations, there's not really an emergency. A true medical emergency is either life threatening or will become so if medical treatment is not given immediately. True medical emergencies most often fall into one of the Big 3 categories described earlier.

A person with a minor injury—a cut finger, twisted ankle, sprained wrist, or skinned knee—can benefit most from what I call "little c.p.r." It stands for *comfort, protection,* and *reassurance.* Even in a real emergency, little c.p.r. has a critical role to play. Little c.p.r. can be useful in many places other than medical emergencies.

The three components of little c.p.r. are important things you can provide if someone is in trouble.

**Comfort.** Make sure the victim is comfortable. Does he need a blanket? Would a drink of water help? (Be sure he can swallow easily.) Is he lying on a sharp rock?
**Protection.** How can you keep the victim from further injury? Are there any immediate threats nearby? Is someone trying to move her when you know she should not be moved?
**Reassurance.** Assume an attitude (I think of it as an "aura"), through words and actions, that lets the victim know he will be okay.

**Teacher Tip**

CPR, like 911, is part of the language of our culture. Even if a child has absolutely no idea that CPR stands for a medical procedure called *cardiopulmonary resuscitation*, she will still connect it with somebody being in trouble.

Ask your group, "What does CPR stand for?" After you've heard several answers, suggest they make up their own terms using those letters as an acronym to help remind themselves what it means if a person is hurt.

Then introduce the concept of little c.p.r. Begin with something like, "A doctor or nurse will tell you CPR stands for *cardiopulmonary resuscitation*. Today we're going to learn another way to use those three letters to help in an emergency: *little* c.p.r., which stands for comfort, protection, and reassurance."

## protection

Right here is a good place for role-play, which can go something like this:

**Comfort**
Have individuals in your group practice giving comfort to another individual. If they feel silly pretending to give comfort to another living being, have them try it with a toy stuffed animal at first. Be sure to remind them that when an actual emergency occurs, they'll need to do all they can to help and forget any self-consciousness.

**Protection**
Simulating protection should be easier. The main thing is to keep others in the vicinity from doing anything that could make the person's situation any worse. Suggesting the rescuer act like a guard dog or policeman can get the ball rolling.

Eventually, you need to talk with your group about exactly how they would keep a well-meaning but uninformed bystander away from an injured person. It's a whole lot easier for an adult be assertive in this situation than it is for a child. This is, of course, another good role-playing opportunity.

**Reassurance**

At first, this concept can be difficult to distinguish from comfort. The importance of making the victim comfortable shouldn't be that hard a concept to understand. Keeping an injured person warm and dry and protected from noise and people who may be staring at the scene makes sense. But in this case, reassurance means a way of behaving toward the victim, especially while you are interacting with her. The rescuer needs to "radiate an aura" designed to convince the injured person she's going to be "just fine."

This may require a certain amount of acting, but it has a very important psychological effect on everyone involved—including the rescuer. The rescuer needs to believe things are going to get better, because he is there and is helping.

reassurance

Now that you have a better understanding of little c.p.r., here is a true story that should reinforce the concept.

## the story...

Jeff and his father enjoyed rollerblading together. Since they lived on a cul-de-sac, there was little traffic. The pavement in front of their house was smooth—perfect for skating fast and performing cool moves while zooming down the street.

At 13, Jeff sometimes forgot to wear a helmet while skating, but Dad was a doctor and should have known better. This day both of them left their helmets at the house. It was a mistake they would regret.

While rollerblading helmetless out in the street, Dad hit a patch of sand and slipped. His head slammed hard into the curb, and Jeff heard his father shout with pain.

Skating over to him, Jeff saw Dad holding his head. Blood was oozing between his fingers and hair. When Dad removed his hand from the wound, Jeff saw a powerful spurt of blood from Dad's head. Not good!

Think about this story, and consider how you might analyze this as a situation in which little c.p.r. was just about the only option for Jeff. Let's look at the many factors to be considered here:

- Is it safe to help?
- Is the victim breathing?
- Does he have severe bleeding?
- Does he have a possible head injury?
- Could his neck or spine also be injured?
- Is help nearby?
- What can the rescuer do to make things better for the victim?
- Is it going to be difficult for the rescuer to handle his emotions in this situation?

Little c.p.r. is a very important concept, which is why it gets a whole chapter. Sometimes, giving little c.p.r. is all a child can do to help in an emergency situation, so it deserves special emphasis.

If your group learns only two things during their entire WEMA experience, strive to make those contacting 911 and little c.p.r. Both these skills are easy to understand and execute; both lend themselves to lots of playing of the "what-if" game.

## ...the rest of the story

Mother was inside the house, saw Dad fall, and ran out to help. She had foresight enough to bring a roll of paper towels, which she used to staunch the bleeding.

Though it might have been a mistake, she had Dad sit in the front seat of the family car while she took him to the nearby Emergency Room.

Except for a few stitches (along with joking comments from his fellow physicians), Dad was fine.

**Teacher Tip**
Place one of your group members in this situation (ask for a volunteer and you may have more than enough), then see what she would try to do if this were her father. Try this scenario 2 or 3 times. I believe you'll find each rescuer does just about the same thing. In some situations, all a rescuer can do is give little c.p.r.

It may also be appropriate to combine this concept with an emphasis on prevention. It's important for kids to learn what they can do to prevent potential accident situations, but also to be brave enough to speak up to a person who has the power to remedy the problem before it becomes an emergency.

# Notes:

# Injuries, Etc.

## And How to Respond

# Breathing

## the story....

It was lunch time at a rural public school in the mountains of western North Carolina. Thursday was a favorite day with the boys in this particular third grade class; Thursday was hot dog day.

The boys were using their wristwatches to time people who entered their "hot dog race." The teachers didn't like the boys doing this, but the boys were at a table by themselves; the girls in the class were together at another table.

"On your mark, get set, go!" said one boy with a stopwatch, as the first two contestants began cramming hot dogs into their mouths. Everyone was having a great time watching—until they noticed one of the boys had quit eating and was grabbing at his throat.

Quickly, another boy asked him if he was all right. The terrified choking victim vigorously shook his head "No!" as his face began to turn bright red. He fell out of his chair and on to the floor.

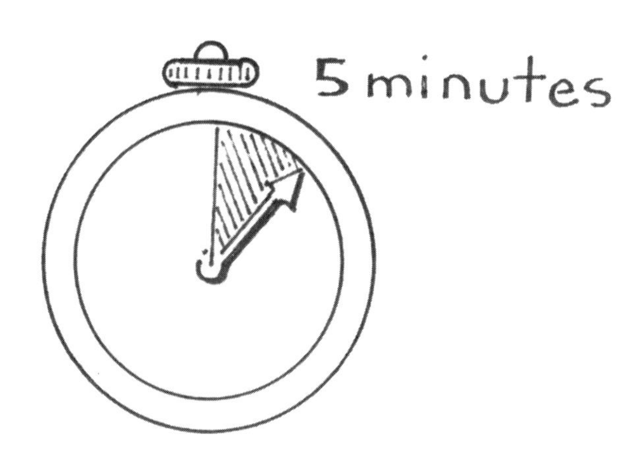


A*s natural as breathing.* We've heard that phrase countless times, but what does it really mean? We each breathe in about 13 pints (just over a gallon and a half) of air every minute of our lives, so breathing must be fairly important, right?

Breathing is the first of the Big 3. Humans require a certain amount of air in their bodies at all times if they are to remain functional. What we call "air" is a mixture of several gases, mainly nitrogen and oxygen. The oxygen is necessary for transferring material to and from the cells, thus keeping us alive. But that's not all. There must be an *exchange* of air as well. Waste products from the body (mainly in the form of carbon dioxide) are removed upon exhalation. Simply put, air goes in and out; blood goes round and round; oxygen is good! Without oxygen, human tissue—most notably brain tissue—can't operate, and death occurs within minutes.

No Breathing
\+ 5 minutes
= Permanent Brain Damage

If a person isn't breathing, we must do everything in our power to change that situation. We have roughly 4 to 6 minutes to take care of the problem. After that, the brain will be permanently damaged.

Sometimes it's obvious that a person isn't breathing. They may have been underwater, trapped in a tunnel cave-in, or buried in a snow avalanche. Ambient smoke or other fumes could have been the cause, or dangerous gases may have been inhaled, sometimes intentionally.

At other times, an unresponsive or unconcious person is found on the ground, and the rescuer has no clue as to what's wrong. Perhaps the rescuer, or a witness, saw what happened and surmised that a fall or blow to the head caused unconsciousness. There could be spinal involvement and damage, in which case tilting the head, even a little, might cause paralysis or death.

> **Teacher Tip**
> Remember: it *must* appear to be safe for a rescuer to enter the scene, lest he also become a victim. This is especially true when dealing with a non-breathing, unresponsive person.

## Questions & Answers

**How can I tell if someone's not breathing?**

As you check the scene for your own safety, also look for clues as to what might have happened. Was the victim found at the bottom of a swimming pool or floating face-down in a lake? If so, she's obviously not breathing and, if not already dead, will be so in a few minutes unless you can start her breathing on her own or can breathe for her until EMS arrives with oxygen. Even then, it may be too late.

At other times, you can't tell. One strategy is to do what the Red Cross has been recommending for years: *look, listen, feel.*

*Look* for movement, especially around the throat and chest. *Listen* for coughing, crying, talking, or any other sound. If you can't hear anything, place your ear next to the victim's mouth or nose and listen for any air exchange. Cover your other ear with your hand to keep out extraneous sounds that could prevent you from hearing the thing of greatest importance: breathing.

*Feel* for air exchange while you're listening, with the very sensitive nerves on the inside of your ear. All of this must be done as quickly as possible, so practice on one another, on members of your family, even on your dog!

**If the victim isn't breathing, what am I supposed to do?**

First, you must establish an airway. There must be a clear path from outside to inside to outside. How do you do this? There are numerous techniques, some better than others, depending upon the injury. As the teacher, you should either know these already, learn them before demonstrating and/or practicing them with your students, or have an expert demonstrate and supervise the practice. Both the American Red Cross and the American Heart Association have excellent courses where you can learn the techniques.

**Okay, I've learned all this stuff about "opening airways," and I still can't get any air inside my victim. What then?**

Usually you have about 5 minutes from the time breathing ceases until irreversible brain damage occurs. If you don't first establish an airway and supply sufficient oxygen to the victim, he will end up with brain damage or he'll die. This important point was stated above, but it's worth repeating.

**I've heard asthma and allergies can cause breathing problems. Anything I can do if that should happen?**

You're right—in most cases, the victim will tell you he has asthma, ate something that causes him to have breathing difficulties (peanuts, for instance), or was just stung by a bee. Unless you have the proper medication and know how to use it, your victim could be in serious trouble.

Call 911—*right now!*—and give a description of the problem and your exact location. The 911 people know how serious this can become, so they'll be there as soon as possible. Make the person comfortable, keep close watch on his breathing, be ready to breathe for him, and give lots of little c.p.r.

**Here are some "what-if" situations to consider.**

- Dad pours charcoal lighter fuel onto hot coals on the grill, and flames explode and hit him in the face. You hear him yell and find him rolling in the yard with his hands up to his mouth.
- Neighborhood boys spray some sort of aerosol material into paper bags, then breathe it to "get high." One of the group frantically rings your doorbell, begging for help.
- While babysitting a small child, you leave her in the tub to answer a phone in the next room. When you return, the child is underwater.
- While on a mountain bike ride over a very narrow and rocky trail, the biker in front of you hits a rock and is thrown over the handlebars. You stop, ready to ask, "Are you all right?" when you see your companion crumpled in a heap, not making a sound.

## ...the rest of the story

The boy on the floor is not moving, and his face is becoming very dark. The other children, realizing something is wrong, run to the teacher's table, asking for help.

One teacher yells out, "Call 911 right now!" Another, not recognizing the boy isn't breathing, turns the boy over and screams at him, "Please, open your eyes and talk to me!"

It's now been 2 or 3 minutes since the child took his last breath. A teacher, trained in CPR, starts pushing on the boy's chest. Someone asks, "Is he breathing?"

With that, a third teacher puts her mouth on the choking boy's mouth and tries to breathe. No air goes in. She tilts his head back and tries again—nothing.

By the time EMS arrives, 10 minutes after being called, the boy is dead. True story.

### Surveying the Scene

The rescuer *must always* ask:

- Is it safe to help?
- Is the victim responsive?
- Is he having trouble breathing?
- If I move him, could this make matters worse?
- Do I need to breathe for him?
- Can I send someone for assistance?

**Teacher Tip**

There's a lot of material here for a good session on choking prevention and for recognizing when someone has gone within seconds from happily eating lunch to not breathing. This is also a great opportunity for a session on learning techniques for establishing an airway. Bring in an expert trainer from your local EMS or fire department if necessary.

## Notes:

# Notes:

# Bleeding

## the story...

Chain saws are certainly one of the most dangerous power tools a person can buy at the home improvement store. Last Saturday, Dad bought a big, powerful model and now is out in the yard, learning how to use it. You are standing nearby, hoping he doesn't do something wrong.

Dad pulls the starter cord and the chain saw roars to life. As he revs it up and begins ripping into a large section of a fallen tree, the blade hits a knot in the wood, and the saw jumps out of Dad's hand , sinking into his upper leg.

Bleeding is the second of the Big 3. Whether it's your blood or someone else's, bleeding seems to terrify people. Everyone knows how important blood is and how it circulates in the body, but seeing it leaking out of the body can have an incredible psychological effect on some rescuers. Red is a vivid, important color that's a special part of emergency care. When a rescuer sees blood, or when the victim or bystanders see it, it's time to take action right away.

Our ancestors, way back when, must have sensed a direct connection between that red, sticky stuff and imminent death. If a lot came out, either from the body of a person or from the animal they were hunting, it meant things were just about over.

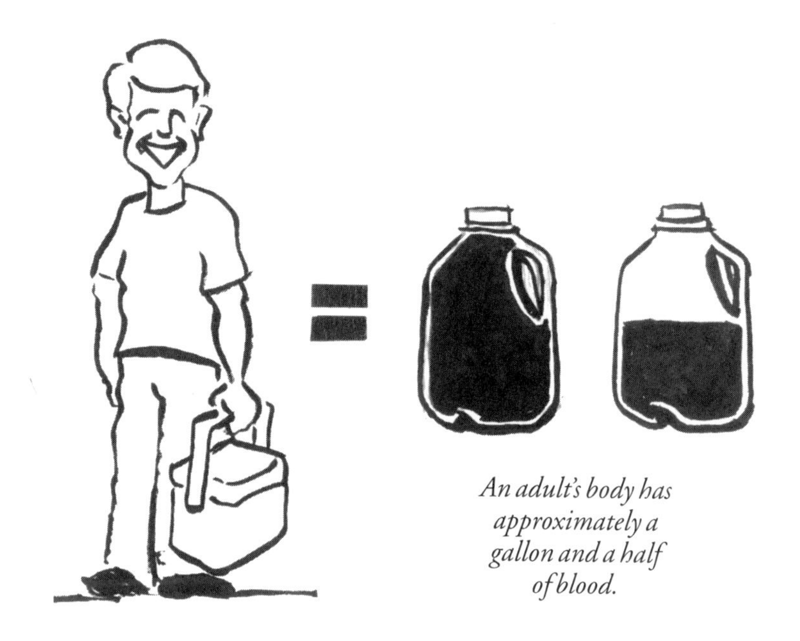

*An adult's body has approximately a gallon and a half of blood.*

**Teacher Tip**

Play with the symbolism of RED here.

- The red, white and blue colors of the U.S.flag.
- Stop signs and stop lights are always red.
- When someone's mad, they're said to "see red."
- To "red-shirt" an athlete has a special meaning to a team.

I'll bet you can think of many others, as will your group.

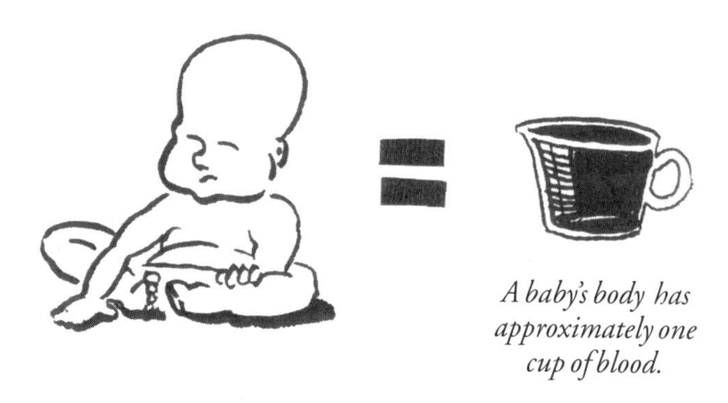

*A baby's body has approximately one cup of blood.*

## Questions & Answers

**How much blood do we have?**

A typical adult has between 5 and 6 liters (a liter is roughly one quart, so that works out to a gallon and a half). A newborn baby has around one cup of blood.

**How much blood can we lose without having a problem?**

When a person donates blood, they lose what is called a "unit" (roughly one pint, or about a soda bottle and a third). Pour out the contents of a typical water bottle, and you'll get a good idea of how much blood a healthy adult can lose before having a problem. As you'll see, it's a lot of blood!

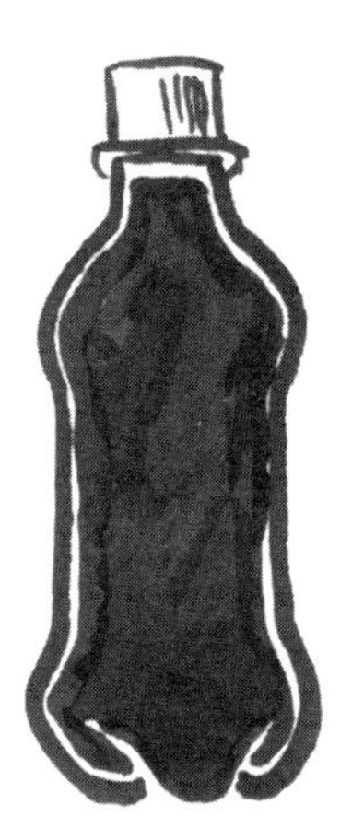

*A unit of blood is equal to one pint, or about a soda bottle and a third.*

**What do I do to stop external blood loss?**

1 *Find the leak.* It may mean removing clothing or cutting it away to find the actual spot.

2 *Apply firm direct pressure* over the leak, using a towel, cloth, bandage, or other absorbent material.

3 *Hold until the bleeding stops.* This could take 10 to 15 minutes. If possible, also raise the bleeding area above the level of the heart.

### What about using a tourniquet?

When bleeding is severe, it must be stopped or the person will die. Tourniquets are used only in such cases, which are rare. To make a tourniquet, wrap a wide band of material, such as a T-shirt, above the area that's bleeding. Slip something that can be used to twist the tourniquet tight (a screwdriver, pipe, or strong stick) under the band and tighten it until the bleeding stops. Since this technique stops all bleeding, there is a good chance the limb will die and need to be amputated.

### What if something is accidentally amputated?

1 Clean the cutoff part by washing it in water clean enough to drink.

2 Wrap the part in a dry, sterile bandage.

3 Cool the part. Put it in a waterproof plastic bag, and submerge the bag in ice water (ice water, not a bed of ice). Take the whole thing with the victim to the hospital. They may be able to reattach the part. (More about amputations in *When Parts Come Loose*, p.112.)

### What does it mean when someone says "Treat for shock?"

Shock is a word that has lots of different meanings. In the situations we anticipate in this program, it can mean one of two things:

1 **The victim responds emotionally to the injury.** Generally, the victim either faints or becomes very active. Another name for this is *acute stress reaction*. Both problems are self-correcting; the injured person soon returns to normal. Little c.p.r. can be very helpful here.

2 **The body compensates for losing too much blood.** In this case, a rescuer can do little except recognize that serious blood loss has occurred and that the victim needs immediate professional assistance. This kind of shock, called *volume shock*, is characterized

by rapid pulse and rapid breathing. The person may act very confused, also becoming weak and chilled as time passes.

Keeping the person warm and giving little c.p.r. can help, but neither will do anything to increase the low blood volume. Raising the victim's feet can be of some value, but must *not* be done if a head injury is suspected, or if the victim has an injury to the legs or pelvis.

**Seeing blood makes me dizzy. Can I do anything about that?**

*If you don't have rubber gloves, plastic bags over your hands are better than nothing.*

First of all, this is a normal reaction in an emergency situation. In this case, the acute stress reaction is in the rescuer.

Taking a deep breath, perhaps saying a prayer, then doing the best you can will usually get you through the situation. If you feel you're going to faint, back against a wall and slowly sit yourself on the ground. Difficult as it might be, you need to recover and help.

**Can I get sick from someone else's blood touching me?**

Probably not, but you can protect yourself by putting on rubber gloves, glasses (sunglasses will work), and a rain jacket before dealing with serious bleeding. Gloves should be in your first aid kit, but plastic bags on your hands are better than nothing. Afterward, wash thoroughly as soon as possible.

A cut on the head or lip, a bloody nose, blood in the mouth or running down from the hair line into the eyes and mouth are very upsetting to the victim—and look horrible to the person trying to help. Cuts on the head tend to bleed profusely.

These kinds of injuries can look a whole lot worse than they are. Provide lots of little c.p.r., check for the source of bleeding, give firm and well-aimed direct pressure to the place causing the problem, clean up the blood, and then see what needs to be done next.

**How do I take care of a bloody nose or nosebleed?**

Have the person sit down, lean forward, and pinch her nostrils together for about 5 minutes. If there's still a problem, have her gently blow her nose (or sniff with force) to remove the clots, then repeat the first step. If nose drops are available, these can be sprayed into the nose and may help stop the bleeding.

## ...the rest of the story

Remember the chain saw story that started this section? Messy as it was, this was actually a simple one to treat. Here's how.

Stop the chain saw. Most new ones stop immediately when the operator releases the handle.

Sit Dad down, then find the place that's bleeding. Dad may need to take off his pants, or you may need to tear or clip the material away with scissors so you can see your "target" better.

Using a shirt, a towel, or something else absorbent, stop the bleeding with well-aimed

## ...the rest of the story

direct pressure. Use tape to hold the bandage in place, and call for help (911).

Keep watching to see that the bleeding has stopped. If it persists, add more material and pressure.

Uh-oh! Did you forget your gloves, glasses, and rain jacket? Were they needed to protect you in this case or not?

## Notes:

## Notes:

# Bumped Heads

## (Head, Neck, & Spinal Injuries)

*Don't move the victim! She could have a spinal injury.*

### the story...

Trampolines—all you need to say is that word, and some people start bouncing around right there on the floor! That was certainly true for Ellie and her sleep-over buddies one Saturday morning in April, when they went out in the backyard to enjoy the early spring sunshine.

Ellie's parents had a rule for the trampoline. Nobody was allowed to be on it unless there were at least four "spotters" on the ground. This, they said, was because somebody could miss a bounce and fall from the trampoline onto the grass.

Rachel called "First!" so the other girls took their positions while she climbed onto the tramp.

Up and down, up and down, Rachel established a rhythm that would take her high enough to do her famous double back flip.

Just then, Ellie's new puppy ran out the door, barking and nipping at her feet. For just a moment, Ellie bent down to play with the dog, not suspecting that Rachel would twist and fall at the very spot she had been protecting until her little dog appeared.

Rachel's head banged into the metal railing as she tried to complete her stunt. She fell to the ground and, scaring the puppy, lay very still at Ellie's feet.

bumped head, the third of the Big 3, must be treated differently than either bleeding or breathing emergencies. When there is severe bleeding or no breathing taking place, immediate recognition and action are of life-saving importance. In the case of head, neck, or back trauma—what we call *neurospinal injury*—there's another issue: extreme care must be taken to prevent any movement.

Is Rachel breathing? Is Rachel bleeding profusely? In addition, the rescuer must also focus on the fact that Rachel may have a head, neck, or spine injury. Rachel's height above the trampoline before she hit its frame, along with the body twist she was doing when she hit, added up to a strong possibility of a serious, life-changing injury. Many head injuries result in permanent neural dysfunction, paralysis, or death.

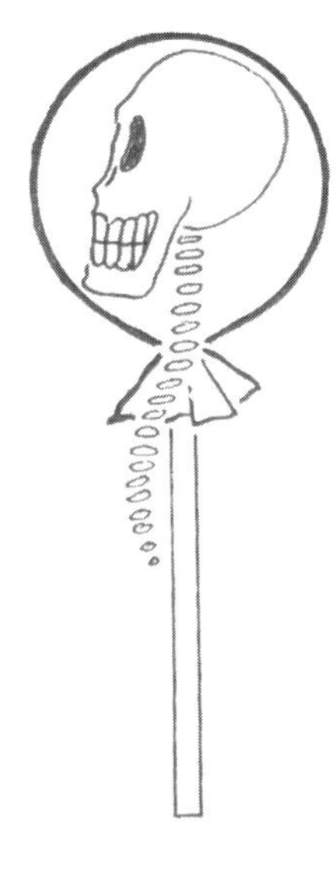

*The head sits atop a thin stalk called the neck—think of a lollipop.*

## Questions & Answers

**What does it mean when somebody's "knocked out"?**

If someone's head has sustained a blow powerful enough to make them lose consciousness for 30 seconds or more, the injury can be quite serious. When trauma causes a person to lose contact with reality, it's an indication they've taken a bad whack to the head. It's also very scary for witnesses and anyone emotionally close to the victim.

**What's so dangerous about being knocked out if you're still breathing all right?**

Trauma to the head—such as Rachel's skull striking the frame of the trampoline—can quickly result in both bruising of the brain and bleeding into the area between the brain and the skull. This can cause pressure that can be life-threatening.

**Why can't we move the person? If they're unconscious, they won't feel any pain and won't know what we're doing anyway, right?**

The head sits atop the thin stalk of the neck—think of a lollipop. Unlike the rest of the spinal column, where the vertebrae are supported by other bones and muscles, the ones in the neck are free to move in all directions. This mobility also makes them very vulnerable.

There are seven bones, or *cervical vertebrae*, in the neck. When there is trauma to the head, these vertebrae are often bent in strange directions, and pieces are sometimes broken off. The jagged edges of the broken pieces can sever delicate nerve tissue, resulting in permanent damage.

That's the reason for this all-important rule: *Don't let anyone or anything move the person's head or neck—period.*

**What if the victim must be moved because of other dangers?**

If the victim must be moved to prevent further injury, such as might result from a car accident in which the car catches fire, the rescuer does the best she can.

**I've checked for breathing and bleeding. Things are okay except the victim is still unconscious. What am I supposed to do now?**

Do two things:

1. Send for help. Make sure you send a clear message that this is a breathing, unconscious victim and that everything possible is being done to prevent movement and retain normal body temperature.
2. Prevent any and all movement.

## Questions & Answers (cont.)

**How can I prevent an adult from moving the person? After all, I'm just a kid.**

It might be difficult, but you *must* make everyone at the scene understand that any movement, especially of the head and neck, could cause permanent damage or death. Here's how to get others to pay attention:

1. Make eye contact with people wanting to move the victim.
2. With all the controlled emotion you can find within yourself, insist that they *not* touch the victim.
3. Remember, they *can* help. Ask them to:
   - Call for professional assistance.
   - Keep the victim warm.
   - Keep other spectators under control.

**Teacher Tip**

Once a young rescuer realizes that *any* head or neck movement can equal death or permanent disability, simple "force of personality" is the most effective persuasion. Simulate and practice this scenario until everyone in your group feels confident they can be effective in a crisis.

**What if the victim is unconscious and not breathing?**

If the victim isn't breathing, respiration is the primary problem. Until an adequate airway has been established and a life-sustaining air exchange is occurring, nothing else matters. An expert trainer can teach useful techniques involving in-line traction on the head and spinal column while gently moving the jawbone perpendicular to the axis of the spine—jutting the jaw. This action positions the tongue far enough away from the victim's airway for rescuers to put air into the victim's lungs, with little or no movement of the head or neck.

> **Teacher Tip**
> Have a Red Cross First Aid instructor or Emergency Medical Technician demonstrate this for you. It's a more effective technique if two rescuers work as a team.

Once it's been determined that the victim is breathing and not in imminent danger, everyone at the scene must understand that further movement of any kind could be catastrophic. In this case, the sheer force of personality of the rescuer can determine the outcome.

## ...the rest of the story

Ellie immediately yelled for someone to call 911 while she bent down to listen for breathing. Rachel began to move around a little, then vomited all over her shirt. Then, Rachel turned her head, spit, and said, "Yuk!"

Ellie broke into happy sobs, but asked her friend to lie still until the paramedics arrived. Everyone could hear the sirens down the street, coming closer— to where, happily, help probably wouldn't be needed.

## Notes:

## Notes:

# Contacting 911

This section looks a bit different from the others, because in teaching and learning how to call 911 we will focus on role-playing. The "what-if" possibilities are endless. If you can teach your students techniques for effectively contacting Emergency Medical Services (EMS), you have performed a valuable service that will last a lifetime.

Here are good questions to ask your group when beginning this section.

- Have you ever had to call 911?
- What did the dispatcher on the other end of the phone say to you?
- What information will be asked for when you call 911?
- What happens if you call 911 and don't actually need emergency assistance?

*When the EMS dispatcher at the other end of the line hears the voice of a child, he is prepared to offer his own version of little c.p.r.*

Every city or county has its own way of dealing with children when they call. It would be a good idea for you to contact EMS* in your area, explain your goals, and find out what your local EMS dispatcher asks when a 911 call comes in to them. Most likely they'll tell you they ask questions such as:

- Where is the accident?
- How many people appear to be hurt?
- What seems to be wrong with the victim(s)?
- What is being done for the victim(s)?

Many communities have what is called an enhanced 911 system. "Enhanced" means the address of the caller's telephone shows up on the EMS dispatcher's computer screen. With a cell phone, this can cause a problem because only the name of the phone company is displayed on the screen.

It's unusual for a child to be the person calling 911. When the EMS dispatcher at the other end of the line hears the voice of a child, he is prepared to offer his own version of little c.p.r. Dispatchers are trained to deal with children, often asking them to stay connected (they'll say, "Don't hang up!") while personnel are dispatched to the injury site.

*Note: when calling EMS for information, don't call 911. Look in the phone book to find your local EMS organization, which has its own number.

### Asking Someone Else to Call 911

Sometimes another person must call 911 while the rescuer is handling the emergency. The designated caller could be an adult or another child. When asking someone else to make the call, the rescuer should

- Make eye contact with the designated caller.
- Speak in a firm, controlled voice.
- Tell the caller exactly what to say to the 911 dispatcher.
- Insist the caller stay on the phone until the dispatcher tells her to hang up.

Not every community has enhanced 911, and/or you may be calling from a cell phone, so it's very important to know exactly where you are. Whether you're in your own home, in the city, or out in the woods, the EMS squad is going to need to find you, right?

**Simulating Emergencies**

Here are some role-playing ideas to jog your thinking and help you prepare by becoming more aware of your location.

1. Pretend you've been in a car wreck. What landmarks do you see here? Any street or road signs? Any big highways or Interstates nearby? If so, sometimes they have special mile markers on the side of the road. How about businesses, such as gas stations or places to eat? Can you describe any cars or trucks parked nearby?

2. Pretend you're on a camping trip. Where is your car located? Does the place where you're parked have a special name? Can you describe your vehicle? What trails did you use to reach this spot? Does this camp site have a special name? How long did it take you to get here?

**Teacher Tips**

- With two cell phones, you can give children the opportunity to actually "talk" a make-believe rescue vehicle to the spot you've designated. This is the type of fun-yet-serious activity that will prepare them for helping in an emergency.
- Some phone companies have special phones they use as training tools. These are connected so they can be used in a school situation, where the teacher is working with young children on how to call and talk on a real phone. Explain to your local phone company that your group is trying to learn correct 911 calling procedures. They may offer you use of their training phones.
- Plan a trip to EMS headquarters. Let the students see and hear actual 911 calls being handled, and let them talk with the dispatchers.

> **Teacher Tip**
> Another useful activity (and one that should involve parents) is for children to compose "verbal maps" of how to reach their houses. This can be written or printed in big type, then posted at the home phone. Add to this other emergency information (for example, allergies, contact information for close relatives, family doctor, etc.), similar to lists you might give a baby sitter, and you have something that could be of inestimable value in an emergency.

Cell phones can literally be lifesavers. However, out in the woods or on the river, calling 911 by cell phone may connect you to a different EMS than the one you had originally tried to contact.

When you go on a trip, quiz your group frequently regarding its location. It will keep everyone in good practice, and most likely they'll all feel safer because of your efforts.

**Here's a final simulation.**

You're not getting a phone signal. What do you do now?

- Send someone for help by herself?
- Should she take another person with her?
- What else does she need to carry along?

Listen to everyone's ideas, give them yours, talk with a cell phone expert, even call one of the phone providers. Also, accept the possibility that a cell phone may not be of any help at all in this particular case.

## Notes:

# Taking Charge

## the story...

Mom has fallen down the stairs after tripping over the vacuum cleaner hose. Her screams for help tore you away from the computer game you and your friend were playing down in the den.

Now, the baby's crying and the dog's running around like mad. To make matters worse, there's a bone sticking out of Mom's arm at a strange angle. There's a lot of blood, and your friend has fainted.

rown-ups are supposed to be the ones to take charge in a emergency. Grown-ups know what to do, and when and how to do it, right? At least that's the image presented to children.

The vignette above illustrates how a simple situation can look very complicated. Instead of taking care of one person with an injury, the rescuer has two people down, a crying infant, and an excited dog. An adult might find that difficult. Could a kid handle it?

**Rescuer's Checklist**

- Take a deep breath, maybe even whisper a prayer.
- Say to yourself, "I can help!"
- Is it safe to enter the scene?
- Start with "A, B, C, C!" (see p. 30)
- Is the injury life-threatening or not?
- Do I need outside help?

The rescuer should know that until competent help enters the scene, it's up to him to see to it the victim is not harmed by others—whose good intentions could make things worse instead of better.

It's easy to tell children to take charge or act tough in an emergency, but some role-play here could pay off handsomely in the event they find themselves actually in charge of a rescue situation. We need to be realistic with children, acknowledging that taking charge of an emergency situation could well be the most difficult thing they've ever done. After it's all over, they may want to cry, throw-up, be hugged, even receive little c.p.r.

Remember, the best way to get good at taking charge is to *practice* taking charge. When creating your role-play scenarios, design scenes where kids must confront well-meaning but potentially dangerous bystanders who want to take over.

*The best way to get good at taking charge is to* practice *taking charge.*

**Here are a few "what-if" ideas to get you started.**

- Dad's on a step ladder in the living room, using an electric drill to make holes in the ceiling to install a new fan. Mother's next door in the kitchen when she hears a yell and the sound of something hitting the floor. She rushes into the living room to find your father has fallen onto the drill, which has stuck right in the middle of his chest. Mother, screaming, wants to pull the drill out, right now! You hear all the fuss and enter the living room. You've learned in a first aid class not to remove an object that has penetrated the body. Your mother doesn't know that and is about to grasp the drill handle. What are you going to do now?
- Your college-age brother is home for the summer. He and his friends are having a rowdy time around your family's swimming pool when his best friend, trying to show off with a fancy dive, hits his head on the diving board. Dizzy and bleeding from his scalp, he paddles to the edge of the pool. His friends, including your brother, are about to hoist him out and take him to get stitches in his head. From your training, you realize that he could have neck or spinal damage, and the best thing to do is to call EMS. Now what?
- Grandad's out in the yard, throwing a stick to your dog. Since it's summer, no one's paying attention to

the big woodpile by the door. In his search for just the right stick, Granddad reaches into the pile of wood. A copperhead snake is seeking shade in that very spot. Grandad and the snake meet, and your favorite relative receives a copperhead bite on the hand. A long time ago, Grandad learned that if you're bitten by a snake you'll die unless you cut an X over the fang marks and suck out all the poison. Right now, he's yelling at you, "Fetch me a butcher knife from the kitchen!" You know what he's going to do and are sure cutting open his hand is probably the worst thing possible. What now?

- A neighbor's son is playing on his bike out in the street in front of their house. A teenage girl who just got her driver's license the day before comes roaring down the street. Seeing the child, the driver reacts by pushing on the brake. Only problem is, she hits the gas instead! The little boy is hit a glancing blow by the car's front fender, sending him off the bike and onto the pavement. The driver exits her car and comes running over to the little boy. You have witnessed this accident and now must act.

Pay close attention to each story as you read it. What are the common threads in each situation? For starters, here are three:

- The rescuer has been trained and has a good idea of what to do and what not to do in each situation.
- In each case, the rescuer is faced with telling an authority figure that what they are about to do is wrong and can make the situation worse.
- Though each of these stories sounds life-threatening, the rescuer can probably make the situation better by doing the right thing.

What other common threads can you come up with? Now, let's go back to the vignette at the beginning of this chapter.

## ...the rest of the story

**Possible resolutions**

- If you're going to ignore something, forget the dog for right now! Mother's worried more about the baby than her arm.
- Your friend wasn't out for long. What he had was an acute stress reaction, and now he's available to help you.
- While you offer little c.p.r. to Mom, have your friend bring in the phone and the baby. Take the baby over to Mom, then call 911 and tell the dispatcher your mother has fallen and broken her wrist. Make sure any serious bleeding is stopped and that baby doesn't touch Mom's arm. Keep an eye on the dog, too, to make sure she doesn't jostle Mom. This has been one heck of a day!

**Teacher Tip**

You'll find that role-playing something this intense takes a lot of energy from you and from your students. If you can't teach every little thing I've listed, do some "triage" of your own. Decide what is truly important for your kids to experience, then cut something out, or add an extra session( see *Nuts & Bolts*, p.156).

## Notes:

# The Big P

*Which illustration on these two pages best describes the* Big P*? Read on to find out.*

## the story...

Randy was a senior in high school, in the same class as your brother. One Saturday morning, he brought over a couple of pieces of music for your brother to hear. They were in a band together, and Randy thought the songs might be something their group would want to practice and play at their next gig.

You and your friend were out in the yard when Randy rode up on his bike. You noted (but didn't mention it to anyone until later) that when you greeted him, he didn't respond immediately, because he was wearing headphones. No helmet, either!

About an hour later, Randy hopped back on his bike, donned his headphones, waved good-bye, and left to go home.

Shrubbery at the front of your house hid your driveway from passing cars. Too late, one of your neighbors saw Randy as he turned out of your drive and into the road.

There was a scream and a horrible crash. Randy's rear wheel had been hit, hurling him onto the hood of your neighbor's car and breaking her windshield.

he "Big P?" No, this isn't a reference to what happens when traveling with children for long periods, then stopping at a gas station to use the restroom. The Big P stands for *prevention*, and it's extremely important.

Prevention should always precede treatment. Proper prevention can well make treatment unnecessary. If only our health care system would embrace this attitude!

**Teacher Tip**

Of course we always should be alert to possible injury situations whenever we're dealing with children. If you're a parent, you probably childproofed your kitchen and bathroom when the little ones started to crawl, right? If you live on a busy street or have a swimming pool at your home, you probably have a high fence and locking gate to keep small children in or out of potentially dangerous places.

One note of caution: Important as prevention is, take care you don't become too preachy with this topic. It's easy for adults to end up browbeating children, especially if there's a pet subject you feel compelled to address.

Couching information about potentially dangerous situations in a role-play activity works much better than admonishing your group to "always be careful," and the lesson is much more likely to sink in and stick with the learner. There are lots of games with what-ifs related to preventing injuries.

## What-If Scenarios

- Choose a spot outside in the grass or inside on a wooden floor that won't be damaged if you stick a nail or open knife into it. In a camp setting, a rustic cabin floor or a swim dock makes a great venue.

Seat your group, then have them take off their shoes and close their eyes. Tell them that with their shoes off, there is danger of a very unpleasant injury to them if they're not very careful.

While their eyes are shut, stick an open pocket knife into the wooden floor. Do the same with a nail. Leave a shard of broken glass in an obvious place. Now ask them to open their eyes and, without leaving their spots, see how quickly they can find these items. You can also add rubber spiders, snakes, fake dog droppings, and/or vomit. (What you're trying to teach is not that vomit or dog feces are dangerous, but to be more observant.)

- Perhaps you're working with a group of young mountain bikers or road bikers, teaching them to check their bikes prior to riding. Buddy them up with another member of the class, and count off A and B. Then have the As in each pair close their eyes while the Bs do something to their partner's bike to make it unsafe—for example, move the chain so it won't work, loosen a quick release, let air out of a tire, or detach a brake cable. (Assure the group that nothing will be done to actually hurt the bike and that they'll have a chance to do something similar to their partner's bike very soon.) Then have the As open their eyes and see how quickly they can find the problems. Switch roles and repeat.
- To add to the game show atmosphere, have little prizes or awards to give out. It's helpful to use a whistle, bell, or bike horn to signal when someone is coming close to a "dangerous" situation, and it adds to the fun.

With each of these activities, hold a debriefing to address the underlying reason for this game. You've just encouraged these youngsters to be "whistle-blowers" or "tattletales," and they may have come from environments where this is not done. Each group member needs to know there's a good reason to speak up and prevent an accident before it happens.

*With the Big P in mind, how many accidents can you find waiting to happen in this picture?*

*What about this one? See any potential accidents that are preventable? Go to p. 167 to see what I found.*

## the story continues...

Randy looks like a bloody mess, your neighbor is out of her car and frantically yelling for help, and you are the only emergency-trained person on the scene. What are you going to do?

**Again, start your survey of the situation with the rescuer's checklist.**

### Rescuer's Checklist

- Take a deep breath, maybe even whisper a prayer.
- Say to yourself, "I can help!"
- Is it safe to enter the scene?
- Start with "A, B, C, C!" (see p. 30)
- Is the injury life-threatening or not?
- Do I need outside help?

**Next, look at what is happening.**

Double check: do we have possible spine, head, or neck injury here?

Is this a time to call 911?

How many people are involved in this situation who will need assistance? (Hint: think about the victim, the driver, your brother, your friend, other witnesses, and yourself.)

**What could have been done to prevent this injury?**

In other chapters, the focus has been on how to respond after the injury happens. Since this is the *Big P* chapter, let's turn our attention to what could have been done to *prevent* this injury. Flip back to the beginning of the story and read it again. What are the obvious, and perhaps not so obvious, actions that might have prevented this situation from being so serious?

**Okay, here are some.**

- Don't wear earphones while riding a bike.
- Always wear a bike helmet.
- Look both ways when entering a street.
- Trim the hedges at the edge of the driveway to open up the line of vision.

**Teacher Tip**

Once again, avoid being overbearing with this section. Couching prevention material in role-playing and what-if scenarios will be more effective than lectures admonishing kids to "always be careful."

## ...the rest of the story

Randy was hospitalized for several weeks with a severe head injury and wasn't able to return to school on a full-time basis for the rest of his senior year. No more band, no more biking, and no college, as yet. Randy's still working on his GED and wishing he'd listened to his mother and worn a helmet. (Based on a true story.)

**Prevention Summary**

- Recognize potentially dangerous situations.
- Be brave enough to say something to someone who can rectify the situation, even if that person is yourself.
- Realize that your advice may be ignored.
- Try hard not to say, "I told you so!" later.

## Notes:

# Notes:

# Broken Bones

*As much as possible, immobilize and protect the suspected break.*

## the story...

"I heard it break, I swear I did!" said your best friend as she looked at her left arm. Yep, the arm did look pretty bad, bent at a strange angle, but you didn't tell her that.

She crashed while the two of you were biking on a trail several miles from where the cars were parked, and the late afternoon sky appeared to hold a thunderstorm. That could include lightning. A messed up arm, bikes to deal with, and a possible lightning storm to boot—not a good combination!

ometimes it's easy to tell when a bone is broken, especially a long bone, such as an arm or leg. Not only does a broken bone hurt quite a bit, it doesn't function normally.

A break or a crack in a bone is called a fracture. If a wrist, knee, or ankle is hurt, it swells quickly and can be so painful that it temporarily cripples the injured person. When a joint is damaged without a bone being broken, it's called a sprain.

Sometimes a bone can look ready to poke itself out through the skin. This can be either 1) the end part of a broken bone or 2) the end of a bone that has pulled away from the joint and is now in a new, strange area. This is called a *dislocation*. If the end of a broken bone actually comes through the skin, it's called an open or *compound fracture*.

> **Teacher Tip**
> Chances are, some of your group have had sprains or broken bones. Involve them by asking
>
> - What caused the injury?
> - Did you hear or feel it break?
> - How were you helped at the scene?
> - Did the hurt place swell up or change color?
> - How long was it before you could use that bone or joint again?

While a broken bone or sprained joint can be unpleasant and painful, it's usually not life-threatening. On the other hand, if one of them belongs to you,these injuries are big deals. Remember how careful we were around head injuries? Let's be just as careful with any broken bone.

**Rescuer's Checklist**

- Take a deep breath, maybe even whisper a prayer.
- Say to yourself, "I can help!"
- Is it safe to enter the scene?
- Start with "A, B, C, C!"
- Is the injury life-threatening or not?
- Do I need outside help?

If something is swollen, painful, and bruised-looking, it must be treated very gently. If the person must be moved, the injury should be splinted or at least immobilized before trying to get the victim to safety. The object is to keep from moving the part that's hurt.

Consider this chapter's introductory story. By itself, the injured arm is not a life-threatening emergency. The arm can be immobilized, and both bikers can walk out to the car. If the bikes cannot be taken along, they can be hidden in the woods and retrieved the next day.

Now add a thunderstorm, and you have lightning, which might be drawn to the metal bikes. Late afternoon means darkness will fall before long. With a wet and injured person who may not be able to ride a bike, an overnight stay in the woods might be the only option, raising the danger of hypothermia, a potentially life-threatening condition in which the body is unable to retain heat.

This situation gives your group some complex variables to think about and introduces two topics which blend nicely with an emphasis on prevention. Hypothermia and lightning strikes are generally preventable problems.

**Teacher Tip**

Splinting a bone or joint is a fairly simple activity and gives your group plenty of opportunities to work with others to create something that prevents movement of the injury. If you need outside professional instruction to help your group to practice this skill, ask an EMT or first aid trainer to demonstrate the correct technique.

To summarize,

- don't move the injured part unless you must.
- make the victim comfortable by arranging for some sort of splint.
- apply lots of little c.p.r.
- secure professional help as soon as possible.

## Questions & Answers

**Can a person tell if a bone is broken or not?**

Swelling and discoloration (like a bruise) are often part of the picture; deformity of the area around the bone or joint are also possible signs of a break.

The person sustaining the trauma may have felt and/or heard a snapping sensation. This is often the case with the long bones of the arm or leg.

While all of those signs could indicate a broken bone, any injury with damage to the skeletal system can be both painful and temporarily debilitating. All suspected breaks, dislocations, or sprains should be handled very carefully. Don't move the victim unless it's necessary to do so for his continued safety.

**Besides not moving the victim, what should I do?**

1 Arrange for transportation if you're able to call 911 and EMS is able to get to you. If not, you'll need to improvise a splint, stretcher, and some means of transport.

2 Keep the victim comfortably warm. The combination of pain and the idea of having been hurt causes most people to become nervous and cold. Some call this state being in shock, while others call it acute stress reaction. In some cases, providing little c.p.r. may be the only thing a rescuer can do to make the situation better.

3 A plastic bag of ice cubes, wrapped in a towel, t-shirt, or other padding, and placed at the site of the injury can reassure the victim and reduce swelling. It also gives you another reason for wanting to keep the victim warm.

**Are grown-ups more likely than kids to have broken bones?**

As with so many things in life, it depends. Elderly people often have lost much of their bone density. Their sense of balance is sometimes impaired. Both of those factors can make for big bones being broken in a fall. This includes the pelvis and the "ball" of the femur (thigh bone), where it fits into the pelvis. Kids, on the other hand, are more prone to breaks in the lower arm, wrists, and fingers.

## ...the rest of the story

It was a long, slow, cold walk, but you managed to immobilize the arm, and the two of you made it out right after sunset. Even though it was summer, there was still a danger of one or both of you becoming hypothermic. Fortunately, you were prepared. Both of you had carried rain jackets and small flashlights in your fanny packs, just in case. Pretty smart bikers!

# Notes:

# Critter Problems

First off, what is a "critter?" Let's say it's any living creature that swims, flies, walks, crawls , or otherwise moves around. Except for the few that feed off humans (mosquitoes, ticks, leeches, and such), most cause problems for us only when they're defending something.

In this chapter, we'll discuss bites and stings—injuries that can be frightening and painful, but are generally not life-threatening.

**Teacher Tip**
Here's an opportunity to educate the kids in your group about bite and sting prevention. In the process, they can learn more about how people relate to animals and vice-versa. Whether you're talking about scorpions, snakes, slugs, or schnauzers, there are loads of myths and misconceptions out there that could be potentially harmful to children and their parents.

Start with questions such as these:

Who here has ever been bitten by a dog? Cat? Other mammal? (It's easy to define mammals in this case—they're animals with fur on their bodies.) How about a snake? Fish? Salamander? Tick? Mosquito?

If you have the time and inclination, it's useful for each group member to tell a brief story about what happened. Then shift the topic a little and ask, "Have you ever been stung by a bee?" (Most stings are from ants, yellow jackets, or wasps, though many call them "bee stings.") You'll have lots of enthusiastic hands waving in the air on this one, along with a swarm of stories about how it happened.

**Questions to think about**

- What were you doing when the animal hurt you?
- Was the animal responding to what you were doing, or did it simply attack you out of nowhere?

Finding out how each bite occurred will probably reveal that the animal involved felt threatened by the child and was protecting itself from harm. During the discussion, help your group realize why each of them was "attacked."

Note that this chapter didn't start off with a story. Your group members will tell their own critter stories, and it's up to you to use those as the basis for this lesson. Children are fascinated by critters, and you're imparting information here that will go with them long after they've left your class.

**More questions to think about**

- Did it cause you permanent harm (physical and/or emotional)?
- In the future, do you think you'll act differently when you're around that sort of critter?

## Questions & Answers

**Lots of people have been bitten by dogs. Is there any way to tell when a dog might bite you?**

One thing you can do is observe dog body language. Is the dog growling or barking? Is it backing away when you approach? Are the dog's ears up? Tail between the legs? Lips curled, showing its teeth? Is the hair on its back standing up? These are some signs that the dog's not happy with you. Respect that, and don't insist on petting the animal. For some reason, it doesn't welcome your attention at the moment.

**What would make a dog act that way?**

You may have surprised the dog while she was sleeping, eating, or looking after her puppies. Perhaps you're in its territory—its yard or house, the place where the dog stays while the owners are away, or even the area in the house where it eats. Sometimes, you may have no warning. Maybe it's sick and wants to be left alone. Dogs are mysterious critters, often hard to predict!

**How can you tell if a cat's going to bite or scratch you?**

Cats will let you know when they want to be cuddled and when they don't want anyone touching them. When they purr, rub up against you, or climb into your lap, you have a pretty good idea what they want, don't you? Cats also let you know if they want to be left alone. If you see a cat's fur stand up on its back, feel it tense up when you try to touch it, or see its claws coming out of the paw pads, put the cat down quickly and gently.

Cat bites can be serious. Long, sharp teeth, loaded with germs, cause deep infections. Hands are the most common spots for cat bites. As with any bite that breaks the skin, wash the area thoroughly for several minutes, then see a physician for professional treatment.

**At night, we sometimes turn on the outside light and watch the opossums eating food we put out for them. Raccoons will sometimes come, too. Are they dangerous?**

Opossums and raccoons can be dangerous to your dogs because they may fight. It's unnatural for a wild animal to come into your yard during the daytime. Should a strange (that is, unknown to you) wild animal be seen, stay away from it. If possible, call your dog into the house immediately.

Rabies, which is fatal in humans if not treated immediately, and distemper, along with some other diseases that affect wild animals, will cause critters that normally avoid humans to wander into a yard. So if you see a wild animal behaving abnormally, call your parents and have them contact the proper authorities.

**I've heard some people are allergic to bee stings. What does that mean, and why is it so serious?**

It's normal to have pain, redness, and swelling when you're stung by an insect. All of that usually goes away fairly quickly—within a few days. However, if a person is stung on the hand, it's *not* normal to have itchy, red blotches (hives) elsewhere on his body and feel his throat tightening so he has trouble breathing. This is called *anaphylaxis,* and it can be life-threatening. Anaphylaxis is uncommon, but for the people who are severly allergic, some insect stings are potentially deadly.

**Okay, I'm with a person who's stung. She starts to have trouble breathing. What am I supposed to do?**

The symptoms of anaphylaxis—hives and difficulty breathing—may occur within minutes after being stung, or it may take longer before the danger signs appear. In the case of an anaphylactic reaction, an injectible drug called epinephrine should be administered by a trained person. Call 911 and let the dispatcher know about the allergic reaction to an insect sting. After that, little c.p.r. and readiness to give rescue breathing to the victim is all you can do. This situation would be unusual, but quite serious.

*The typical reaction to an insect sting is pain, swelling, and redness at the site of the bite. If other symptoms begin to show up later, you are probably dealing with anaphylaxis.*

**What about snake bites?**

Remember the Big P? You shouldn't ever need to worry about snake bite happening to you if you follow these two guidelines: 1) be sure not to touch a snake you don't know and 2) don't stick your hand in a "snakey" place. If someone else is bitten, you need to know if venom has been injected or not. Immediate pain and swelling at the site of the bite tells you the victim has received venom.

If bloody tooth marks and a scared victim are all you see, the bite was either from a nonpoisonous snake or from a poisonous snake that didn't inject any venom. Little c.p.r., along with soap and water to clean germs away from the bite area, should take care of the problem very nicely.

**If it was a poisonous snake bite, what can I do to help?**

Little c.p.r., a 911 call, then more little c.p.r. Though the victim is scared and in pain, it's unlikely that things are as serious as the victim (and you) might think. In this situation, continual reassurance is necessary and helpful.

**What if the bite happens out in the woods, far from EMS help?**

You may be able to walk the person very slowly out to the road, or it may be necessary to arrange for EMS to meet you at the road or to come in to where the victim is. If the bite is:

**On the hand:** Remove rings, bracelets, and watches; the hand will swell very quickly. Keep the bitten hand below the heart. Give liquids in small sips, unless the victim is nauseous. Splint the hand to prevent movement.

**On the foot:** Well, so much for walking the victim out, right? Make her comfortable, give liquids, and see if you can find a way to keep the foot lower than the heart. It would be a good idea to remove the shoe.

**Note:** There are some poisonous snakes—coral snakes, for example—in this country that cause a different reaction. With their bite, look for little sign of trauma at first, then general numbness at the site of the bite, possibly some swelling, headache, and then breathing troubles as much as several hours later. You can find more information on poisonous snakes and their bites on the Internet or at your local library.

**How dangerous are spiders and scorpions to humans?**

Not very. Once again, we're talking about prevention. In scorpion and spider country, don't walk around in the dark barefooted or pick up firewood without looking at what you're doing. Shake out any clothing you left in a pile last night, and look in your shoes before stuffing your feet inside.

If you research these critters, you'll find they're no big deal. Few people ever have problems with spiders and scorpions. While you're at it, check out the myth of the "deadly" daddy long legs, often said to be the most dangerous spider alive. Your research findings will tell you otherwise.

**Dangerous Dogs**

In fatalities from dog attacks reported between 1979 and 1998, the top 10 breeds involved are listed from most reported to least reported:

- Pit-bull type
- Rottweiler
- German shepherd
- Husky type
- Malamute
- Wolf-dog hybrid
- Mixed breed
- Chow chow
- Doberman
- St. Bernard

Source: *The Journal of the American Veterinary Medical Association.*

# Notes:

# Notes:

# What About Burns?

*Gently cool a painful burn with a clean towel soaked in water—ice water, if you have it.*

## the story...

Dad was preparing to barbecue outside on a Sunday afternoon. Just before he started his fire, a thunderstorm moved in and soaked his charcoal—he had forgotten to close the lid on his cooker.

After trying and failing to start the fire, Dad made a major mistake. He sprayed lighter fluid all over his charcoal, and with the can still spraying, lit a match. He was immediately knocked down and backward when the flame exploded the can in his hand.

The can's plastic top popped out, dousing Dad's face and beard with fuel and burning him all around his nose, lips, and tongue.

As you come to his aid, you note he's having trouble speaking and breathing. Your mother and sister are in the kitchen.

Most adults have never dealt with a burn more serious than sunburn, rope burn, or the painful result of spilling hot coffee. Many children and adults may be completely unfamiliar with more serious burns, having no idea how they look, smell, or feel.

The object here is to learn to take care of a burn and not to get hurt in the process. The good news is that most burns are *not* life-threatening! Below is a simple plan that should take care of the majority of burn emergencies.

**Burn Rescue Checklist**

- Stop the fire or remove the source of the burn.
- Send for help.
- Cool the burned area.
- Remove items that might cause a problem.
- Give little c.p.r.

Remember—often burn emergencies involve fire, and the rescuer could easily become a victim. In some burn situations, perhaps the only thing a prudent rescuer could do would be to summon help. Discuss each rescue action for burns within your group.

***First-degree burns*** *are red, painful, and look much worse than they are.*

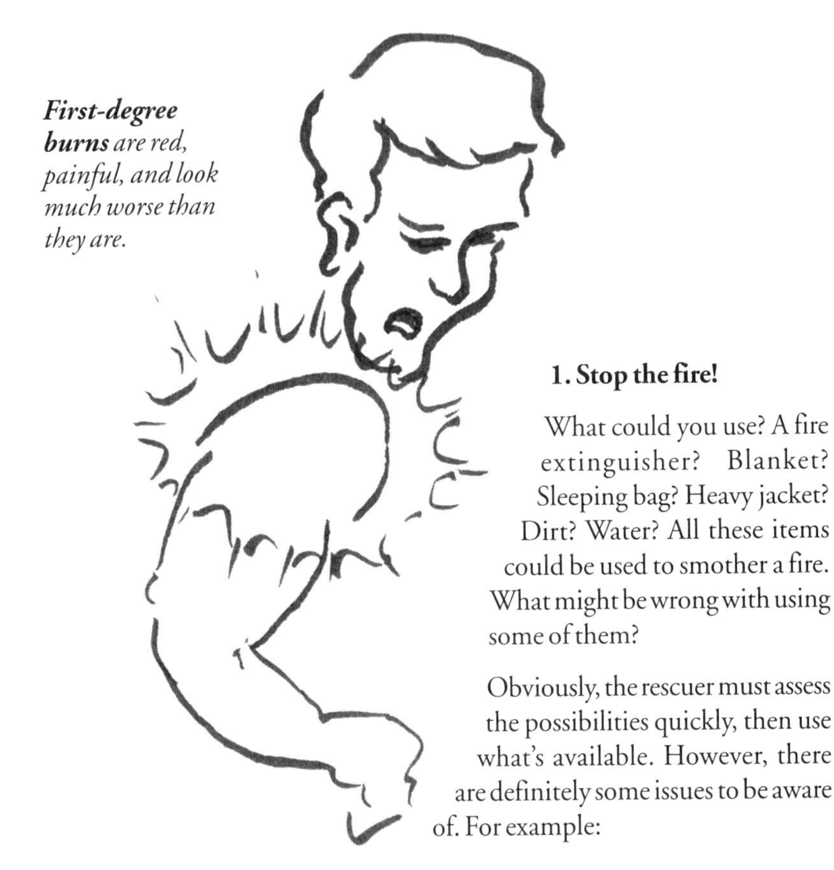

**1. Stop the fire!**

What could you use? A fire extinguisher? Blanket? Sleeping bag? Heavy jacket? Dirt? Water? All these items could be used to smother a fire. What might be wrong with using some of them?

Obviously, the rescuer must assess the possibilities quickly, then use what's available. However, there are definitely some issues to be aware of. For example:

- Dirt can contaminate the wound.
- Some fire extinguishers are only good on certain types of fires, and chemicals can cause further injury.
- The blanket, sleeping bag, or jacket may be made of material that could melt and cause further injury, or it could actually catch fire itself.

**2. Cool the burned area.**

Cooling immediately removes a great amount of the pain associated with a burn, making the situation easier to deal with, both for the victim and the rescuer.

Specifically, what are some ways to gently cool a painful burn? Ice applied directly can cause frostbite and also constricts the blood vessels at the injury site, which keeps the blood from flowing and helping to heal the wound. Instead, use water or something that holds

### The Three Types of Burns

- **First-degree burns** are red, painful, and look much worse than they are. Cool the burn quickly, don't let anything rub against it, and it will soon be no problem. Sunburn is a good example of a first-degree burn.

- **Second-degree burns** are red and have blisters. These look awful and can be very painful. Don't pop the blisters! Cover with bandages of clean material that won't stick to the wound. Don't apply ointments or creams to the burn because these will simply need to be removed when the doctor takes over.

- **Third-degree burns** can look like charbroiled steak—and smell terrible. These are sometimes called *full-thickness* burns and indicate a serious burn has occurred. Since they are deep, it is often said that the nerve endings have been seared, making them less painful than other burns. Don't put anything over the area other than dry bandages that won't stick to the burn. Some of these have a special slick-looking surface on the part of the bandage that touches the skin. Clean, dry clothing can do the job in a pinch.

water, such as a towel or pillow case. Towels soaked in ice water, especially if they have some soap on them, are useful. Placing the person under a cold shower or in a lake helps cool the burn.

***Second-degree burns*** *are red and have blisters. These look awful and can be very painful.*

**3. Remove items that might cause a problem.**

Jewelry is a good example. The burned area's going to swell, making rings and bracelets very tight on the burned place. Don't pull off pieces of clothing or anything else that's stuck on the burned place. Try not to pop any blisters that form.

**4. Apply little c.p.r.**

This is one of the most effective treatments that can be administered in a burn emergency. Explain to the victim what is happening and why. Little c.p.r. is very helpful with burns. Remember: *comfort, protection*, and *reassurance* can make a big difference.

To summarize, moving the person away from the cause of the burn, cooling the burned area, and letting the victim know that help is on the way are three important ways to make the burn victim more comfortable.

**Another potential problem:**
In the barbecue story that began this chapter, the victim had trouble speaking and breathing because the flames hit him full in the face. Chances are, he inhaled some of the heat and it burned the inside of his mouth. Since his breathing seems to be involved, this is a more serious incident than just a simple burn.

What to do here? Maintain an airway and call for professional help. This extra problem is a reminder—that the ABC's *always* need to be dealt with first at the scene of an injury.

***Third-degree burns** can look like charbroiled steak and smell bad, too.*

## ...the rest of the story

Dad was airlifted to the local hospital, where he was treated for smoke inhalation and third-degree facial burns. After several reconstructive surgeries, he returned home.

Mother and Sister, who were in the kitchen when Dad was burned out in the yard, needed care and counseling. They'd never heard Dad scream like that before.

**Teacher Tip**
The Training Officer for your local fire department has some excellent photographs of burns you could show to your group.

## Notes:

## Notes:

# When Parts Come Loose

## the story...

Mike, one of your good friends, is a guitar player, but he's in his garage right now, using a table saw.

Mike's father taught him how to do this safely, instructing him to always wear safety goggles and to use a stick of wood to push lumber past the whirring saw blade.

Mike's in a hurry today, trying to finish a snake cage for a science project. The cage is due tomorrow, and he procrastinated on his project, practicing with his band instead.

You and Mike's younger sister are out in the yard, kicking a soccer ball to one another. It's hot in the garage, and the saw is creating a lot of sawdust, so the garage door is open.

As Mike, bare-handed and without goggles, guides a board along the saw blade, your soccer ball crashes into the garage and strikes his guiding hand.

With a horrible scream of pain, Mike comes running out into the yard. He's holding a bloody hand and saying something about two of his fingers being cut off by the saw!

Your first impulse is to go find the fingers, hoping that a surgeon can put them back on if you get them to the hospital soon enough.

However, from your training, you know there are two people to deal with first—Mike and his sister. What are your priorities at this time?

By now, your group should know the rules for taking care of victims. Quiz them to see how much of the following they can figure out on their own. In a way, this is a test of how well they've learned, so pay close attention.

**Key points to consider in this situation:**

- Massive arterial bleeding is a possibility, and EMS assistance is necessary. Perhaps Mike's sister could help by bringing you the phone to call 911.
- The amputated fingers should be prepared for transfer with the EMS people. See pp. 114-115 for how to do this.
- Both Mike and his sister need attention while you recover and prepare the fingers.
- Little c.p.r. could be very important in this situation.

*Place the body part in a dry plastic bag or water container, then place the container in ice water, or on a layer of ice in a cooler.*

## Questions & Answers

**What am I supposed to do if somebody gets something cut off?**

There are two kinds of accidental amputations, *partial* and *complete*. Regardless of which kind it is, the rescuer needs to:

1 Take care of the bleeding (see *Bleeding*, p. 50) and supply lots of little c.p.r.

2 Rinse off dirt with clean water.

**For a partial amputation**, bandage the injured appendage in place as best you can. Since the part is still attached to the body, you may still have enough blood circulating through the tissue to keep the part alive.

Cover the injured area with a clean and moist dressing, taking care not to let the part dangle or flop around.

For **a complete amputation**, clean both the wound and the body part, bandage the stub, then wrap the amputated part in clean, moist gauze. Place these in a dry plastic bag or water container, then place the container in ice water or on a layer of ice in a cooler.

**Important:** Take care not to bury or cover the body part in ice. This could cause frostbite, preventing the piece from being reattached.

**Rescuer's Checklist**

- Take a deep breath, maybe even whisper a prayer.
- Say to yourself, "I can help!"
- Is it safe to enter the scene?
- Start with "A, B, C, C!" (see p. 30)
- Is the injury life-threatening or not?
- Do I need outside help?

**What do I do if a tooth gets knocked out?**

Good question. A knocked-out tooth is actually a much more likely event than an amputated body part, so to save a tooth, read on.

Every permanent tooth has two main parts—the root, which is below the gum line, and the crown, the part you can see. Most important, when dealing with a knocked-out tooth, try very hard not to touch the root.

If you, or someone more knowledgeable than you, is willing, try to insert the tooth back into the empty tooth socket it came from.

Here are two other strategies that may work, but they must be done specifically according to these directions:

1. If the victim can do this without choking or swallowing the tooth, have her place it inside her mouth between the lower lip and the gum line. Chances are, anyone old enough to have permanent teeth will be able to keep from losing her tooth down her throat or into her lungs.

2. Place the tooth in a covered container with enough milk to cover the tooth (*whole* milk is best). Commercial tooth-preserving solution is available at drug stores, too. If neither is handy, stir a spoonful of salt into a glass of water and drop the tooth in—it's better than nothing. Do not put the tooth in plain water, nor carry it wrapped in tissue or in a dry paper cup. Get both the patient and the tooth to a dentist as soon as possible.

## ...the rest of the story

Mike's fingers were not salvageable. He had to learn to play the guitar with his other hand doing the fretting. Interestingly enough, he became a skilled rock climber, never failing to create a sensation whenever he climbed with others watching him. (Based on a true story.)

## Notes:

# When Something's Just Not Right

## the story...

Grandma was known as a lively, active 78-year-old lady. Her husband of 53 years had died of cancer about 6 months ago, but his death was no surprise to anyone who knew how much he loved to smoke unfiltered Camels.

Grandma sold her place after Grandpa died.

Now living with her daughter, son-in-law, and grandson, she typically walked the family dog each morning along a dead-end dirt road near their home. But lately she'd been complaining about feeling achiness and fatigue. "I don't feel like doing much of anything," was the way she put it.

Her young grandson, an astute observer of people, noted that even when walking the short distance from the front door to the car, Grandma often stopped and to rub her neck and back.

"Something's just not right!" said the grandson one Sunday evening.

Something's just not right!" doesn't sound like a very scientific medical diagnosis. You may not be able to put your finger on it, but you have a gut feeling something is wrong with a person close to you, especially a child or an elderly person.

It's the same sense you get when your dog's not eating with typical enthusiasm, or she's not bounding around the way she usually does, tail-wagging and eyes wide. Something's not quite right. Maybe you could call it "bad vibes."

Now what? Should you call 911 and summon EMS to the scene simply because you don't like the way a person's acting? Maybe so, maybe not. A lot depends upon what you may already know about the victim or can learn on the spot.

**Substance Abuse**

Most of the people a child is going to encounter are ones they know reasonably well, so typically they will be able to notice unusual behaviors. Even so, they may not realize that Uncle Bill's a diabetic, or that Grandpa has heart problems.

While I don't think that most parents are likely to keep such information from a child old enough to attend a WEMA class, the general health problems of family members aren't typically discussed unless one is occurring or imminent. A family member's addiction to alcohol or other drugs is often hushed up. This could be a cause of concern if a child were to encounter a victim (especially a close friend or family member) and not recognize that individual in a life-threatening situation.

*Is the person "with you?" In other words, is he making sense when he talks? If the answer is no, you need outside assistance.*

Here's one checklist physicians use when substance abuse is suspected.

**Warning Signs of Substance Abuse**

- Physical: Fatigue, repeated health complaints, red and glazed eyes, and a lasting cough.
- Behavioral: Personality change, sudden mood shifts, irritability, irresponsible behavior, low self-esteem, poor judgment, depression, and a general lack of interest.

If you are seeing these signs and symptoms for the first time, answering this simple question will help you determine what to do: Is the person "with you?" In other words, is he making sense when he talks? If the answer is no, you need outside assistance.

**Heart Attack**

"Heart attack" (known medically as a *myocardial infarction*) is not just a phrase, it's a relatively common occurrence. At the first sign of one, 911 should be called immediately. Your group can and should learn to recognize the symptoms of a heart attack. Familiarize your group with the most obvious signs, noting that Grandmother might not show the same symptoms as Grandfather, since signs and symptoms differ between men and women.

**Classic heart attack signs and symptoms**

- Squeezing chest pain or pressure
- Shortness of breath
- Sweating
- Tightness in chest
- Recurring chest discomfort
- Pain spreading to shoulders, neck, or arms

**More likely in women**

- Indigestion or gas-like pain
- Dizziness, nausea, or vomiting
- Unexplained weakness, fatigue
- Discomfort/pain between shoulder blades
- Sense of impending doom

### Cardiac Arrest

Cardiac arrest is *not* a heart attack. *Cardiac* means heart and *arrest* means stop. Should someone's heart stop, and they're not in the company of trained and equipped medical personnel or near an Automated External Defibrillator (AED), chances are that CPR alone is not going to prove very effective. AEDs are becoming commonplace in malls, restaurants, theaters, churches, and other places where large numbers of people gather. As more and more people learn about AEDs, many cardiac arrests have been reversed.

**Teacher Tip**

If you are unfamiliar with AEDs , ask someone from the Heart Association, Red Cross, or local fire department to give you a quick run-through. Who knows—they might even let you borrow one for demonstration to your group, or visit and do it for you!

**Stroke**

A stroke is usually caused by a blood clot that passes into the blood vessels going to the brain, preventing adequate blood flow (and therefore oxygen) to the tissues. When you suspect a stroke, call 911 immediately. EMS ambulances carry special drugs that may dissolve the clot, but those drugs must be administered as soon as possible to prevent brain damage.

Now doctors say a bystander can recognize a stroke by asking an individual to do three things:

- smile
- raise both arms
- speak a simple sentence.

If the suspected victim has trouble with any of these tasks, call 911 immediately and describe the symptoms to the dispatcher.

**Signs and Symptoms of Stroke**

- Sudden numbness or weakness of the face, arm, or leg, especially on one side of the body.
- Sudden confusion, trouble speaking or understanding.
- Sudden trouble seeing from one or both eyes.
- Sudden dizziness, trouble walking, loss of balance or coordination.
- Sudden, severe headache with no apparent cause.

**Poisoning**

Signs and symptoms for poisoning are so numerous and varied it is futile to try to list them. So here's where you should trust your intuition: If something seems wrong, check it out! While different poisons affect a person in different ways, swallowed poisons are often slow-acting and the effects reversible if caught early. As of 2003, the American Academy of Pediatrics recommends *not* giving syrup of ipecac to induce vomiting in suspected cases of ingested poisons.

> **Teacher Tip**
>
> Instruct your group to keep both their local and national Poison Control Center phone numbers next to their phones. The United States National Poison Hotline is 1-800-222-1222. Calling this number automatically links you to the nearest poison center. Recreational drugs are considered poisons, so contact this number for overdose information.

**Paying Attention to Sounds and Smells**

So far, this discussion has been only about what you see that is somehow "just not right." How about sounds and smells that cause you to pause and wrinkle your brow or nose a bit?

There's a certain sound made by children playing in groups, one that gives the parent reassurance that everyone's having fun. While it's a bit hard to describe, you know it by its joyousness and spontaneity. Anyone who's dealt with infants recognizes normal baby-type sounds. Unusual sounds of any kind need immediate investigation. If it doesn't sound right, chances are that something's amiss.

The same is true of smells. It might be smoke, or a "chemical" smell that doesn't fit the place. The smell of human waste from a confused adult with slurred speech might signal a stroke. Strange smells of another sort could mean people experimenting with inhalants of some kind. If it smells wrong, look for the source.

## ...the rest of the story

While depression often accompanies loss of a spouse, and/or an abrupt change in living conditions, Grandma seemed to be physically tired, as well. Walking even a short distance seemed to wear her out much more than it should have.

Hard-headed and independent as Grandma was, her family convinced her it would be smart to see her doctor. After they described her lethargy and the rubbing of her neck/back muscles, results of blood tests indicated she'd recently sustained a mild heart attack.

After a simple surgical procedure was performed to repair and support the blood vessels near her heart, Grandma returned home. For the next several months, she attended supervised exercise programs for people recovering from heart-related problemss. She also changed her diet to make it more "heart-healthy."

Thanks to the perceptiveness of her grandson, the two of them are now taking long walks with the dog.

Perhaps the best we , as teachers and students, can do is to become sensitive to signs of problems—like poisoning, drug abuse, heart attack, and stroke—that could result in unexplainable behavior or unconsciousness. Awareness that something's "just not right" may make a difference and even save the day!

## Notes:

# When It's Hard to Communicate

## the story...

This really happened. It was a weekday afternoon in early December. I was driving home on I-26 near Asheville, N.C., when I was confronted with a strange sight. Right there, lying the middle of the highway in front of me, was a body!

A nurse, on the way to his job at a local hospital, had been first on the scene. He stayed with the young woman's body, assured me he was in control, and suggested I check the others who had been in the car with her.

Nine people, including a 3-year-old, had been crammed into an old Ford Mustang. When the Mustang's rear end was hit by another driver, it threw the woman out of her rolled-down window and onto the asphalt, killing her instantly.

Because the car was so small, all the passengers were packed very tightly into the front and back seats. One of those passengers was the woman's boyfriend, José, who knew very little English. Everyone else in the car was from the local area, and though very shaken, seemed to be fine.

hat if your victim or victims are hard-of-hearing, blind, or don't speak your language? How can you help—or *can* you help?

Don't be surprised if your victims refuse your help at first. After all, you're "just a kid," a "baby sister," or "a child who's getting in the way." You may need to use your "force of personality" to convince them you really *are* able to help.

Use this story, or create one of your own, to place your group in situations in which communication is difficult. Role-playing allows everyone in your group to experience the frustration of not being able to communicate, then come up with options for dealing with unforeseen problems. You might try a situation in which the only other person on the accident scene (other than the victim) acts as if they cannot speak or hear. What should you do? Can you use hand signals? What seems to be most effective?

## ...the rest of the story

Once the fire trucks, EMS units, and rescue helicopter arrived, I was free to assist the others in the wreck. Thanks to the generosity of strangers on the scene, I was able to place everyone in a warm car and provide blankets for those who were chilled.

José now became my personal problem. Though he wasn't hurt, José sensed that things were very bad for his girlfriend. With my limited Spanish, I did my best to offer José little c.p.r., but was unable to find anyone more fluent to assist me—or José.

Ask your group what each of them could or would have done for José if they'd been in my place that day.

# Notes:

# After It's Over

**To the Teacher**

The goal of this training is to teach kids how to react in emergency situations. We hope the outcome is positive—but what if it goes the other way? It's entirely possible that some time or another, one of your students will deal with an emergency that turns out badly.

As you may know from hearing about divorce cases, children sometimes blame themselves for events that are not their fault. This can also happen when a child is involved in a rescue situation that doesn't end well. Disbelief, guilt, anger, and anxiety are some of the feelings one of your group may experience when his efforts to help are not successful. If the victim is a close relative or friend, these feelings are sometimes magnified to the point of despair. The child then becomes an emotional victim who can himself benefit from skillfully used rescue techniques. A responsible adult can play an important role by listening and talking with the youngster and offering reassurance intended to make him feel a bit better about the outcome of the emergency.

A hurting child needs to know the world is still safe for her, that time has a way of making things better, and that life is going to be fun again—though it may take a while. Let her know she is loved and among family and friends who will be there to listen and take care of her, no matter what.

Just as we admonish rescuers to be focused on the emergency at hand and try hard not to show emotion, a person offering counseling to a rescuer who feels he has failed should be able to appear somewhat detached from the incident and keep from "losing it" during this time. This may make it seem like acting, but let's face it; acting is a big part of life. Think about it—if you had a heart condition, you certainly wouldn't want your cardiologist to come into the examination room waving an EKG strip and exclaiming, "Your heart report is terrible! You're a complete mess!" Likewise, you're not going to be an effective counselor for a distraught child if you lose control of your emotions.

What follows is a story for you, the teacher, suggesting a situation similar to one you might encounter in the future.

*Children sometimes blame themselves for events that are not their fault. This can also happen when a child is involved in a rescue situation that doesn't end well.*

## the story...

Bob was 13, in the 7th grade, and loved riding bikes—mountain bike, road bike, or BMX. He spent almost all of his non-school hours either riding or working on bikes.

For the last three summers, Bob had enjoyed camping and mountain biking at a summer camp in the North Carolina mountains. At the camp, he had learned what to do if someone was injured in an accident.

He never expected his dad Rod would need his help one Sunday afternoon, when they were biking down a busy street about a mile from their home. Rod was riding not 10 feet ahead of Bob when a car flew out of a side street on their right. The driver, ignoring the stop sign, struck Rod, sending him and his bike into the trunk of a large oak tree on the other side of the road.

Dismounting immediately, Bob ran to his dad's side. Rod, thrown from his bike, lay twisted and very still at the base of the oak. Without touching his father, Bob started to check the medical emergency ABCs he'd learned at the camp.

"Dad's not breathing!" Bob said out loud, even though no one was around. Out of the corner of his eye, he could see traffic stopping and people talking excitedly into cell phones. Their agitated voices were making it difficult to hear, but Bob could see Rod's face turning dark purple.

By now, several adults were surrounding him, including one older man who attempted to move Bob away from his father. "No!" shouted Bob. "Leave me alone! Don't touch him, either! His neck may be broken, and you could kill my dad!"

Very carefully, Bob unsnapped the chin strap on Rod's helmet, hoping that might let him breathe. It worked!

An ambulance with paramedics was now at the scene. Through his tears, Bob told the paramedic about his dad being knocked off of his bike and hitting the tree with his body. He could still hear that sound in his head and knew he would not forget it any time soon.

Not every story has a happy ending. Rod died on the operating table, from a ruptured aorta. Internal bleeding, caused by the force of his body smashing into the oak, had left his heart with no blood to circulate to the rest of his body.

Let's move ahead now, a few weeks into the future. Life goes on. Except for Bob, his family, and Rod's close friends, things are back to the way they were before the bike accident.

Bob returned to school by the end of the second week

after the tragedy. He had been brooding in his room several hours each day and, when he emerged, his eyes were red from crying. His mother thought it best for him to resume his normal activities.

She has asked *you* to talk to Bob privately, hoping that an old family friend could detach from the situation enough to help her only son regain his composure. What an awesome responsibility!

**Counseling the Rescuer: Where, when, and how do you start?**

**Where** is important—the place you meet could be crucial. You might offer that choice to Bob, letting him determine where he'd be at ease. After a movie, over a meal, during a bike ride or hike, or while traveling to or from one of these activities. This, of course, comes after he's agreed to meet with you in the first place. Though you may feel more comfortable having another adult along, it might be better for this to be one-on-one.

**When** can mean at least two things:
**1** Time of day
**2** Time passed since the accident

Significant people in Bob's life—mother, family physician, school counselor—may have different ideas about when to approach him. I tend to go with the person who knows him best, his mother. She would also probably know the best time of day for this meeting.

Now for the biggie: **How?**

Please note that I haven't called this a "talk" but have referred to it as a "meeting." Though part of your role is to initiate conversation about what has happened, perhaps you could best help by doing a lot of listening, trying very hard not to interrupt or correct Bob, even though the things he describes might not jibe with what you know or have heard regarding this trauma.

One idea is to begin by acknowledging, up front, that talking about the incident may be difficult for Bob. Then, ask him to describe the day of the accident for you. You could say that you've heard a lot of stories but wanted to hear it from the person who would probably know best. No need to indicate that you realize that Bob was the last person to see his dad before the accident. Both of you know that.

Bob may be very angry. "The 911 people could have been more careful!" "God should not have let this happen!" "Why my dad?"

He may feel both frustration and guilt. "I should have called for help quicker!" "I could have unsnapped his helmet faster!" "I shouldn't have begged him to go riding with me!" "It was all my fault!"

Fear can easily overtake a person when stress has weakened his emotional defenses. "I don't want to go by that place any more! I'll never ride a bike again!" "What

*Helping a child rescuer who was unable to save the victim in an emergency can make a huge difference in the life of that child.*

if someone else in my family is killed? What would I do then? What if I get killed?"

These and other thoughts or statements could occur during your meeting. How would you respond? *Could* you respond, or would you find someone else who was willing to help? Here's a mnemonic device from Tricia Williams at the Heart Songs Grief Counseling Program in Hendersonville, N.C., to use as a guideline when counseling a grief-stricken child.

**ADAPT**

- **A**ccept the person's feelings as they are, not as you might like them to be.
- **D**emonstrate your acceptance of these feel ings by listening, then sharing your own grief. This lets the child know that others are grieving with him.
- **A**llow the child to express anger, fear, denial, despair, guilt, and anxiety.
- **P**rovide a reassuring environment, maintain a routine, and offer a feeling of security for the child.
- **T**alk with him in an honest fashion, attempting to answer his questions—or promise you'll find the answer for him somehow.

Schools have counselors, the clergy could be helpful, your EMS director will know of professionals who debrief personnel after critical incidents, and there are books and journals that address this situation. Know that help is out there and that others have been down this road before. Helping a child rescuer who was unable to save the victim in an emergency can make a huge difference in the life of that child.

## Notes:

# Appendix

# Teaching Then and Now

It's been said that if a teacher from the Civil War era was suddenly placed in front of a class being taught between 1960 and 1980, the students wouldn't have noticed much difference. In both time periods, the scene would have looked something like this:

The teacher stood in the front of the room, students were in rows of desks, and the teacher talked, asked questions, wrote on the chalkboard, assigned homework, passed out tests, took up the tests, examined the tests, and then returned them with a grade and/or trenchant comment written in red pencil. That was it!

Please don't repeat this type of teaching. Don't insult and abuse your kids by "teaching" in that manner. You can do better. If you want your group to really absorb this information and be able to use it when necessary, you *must* do better.

**Consider a Different Approach**

For a semester exam in biology, the professor rolled into class a wheelbarrow full of cabbage leaves. He dumped the leaves in the middle of the laboratory floor and made one statement: "You have 2 hours to tell me all you know about these leaves." Then he left the lab.

A great deal of learning went on during those two hours, I can tell you, and you're learning from that lesson right now as you read this book.

No two people learn—or teach—exactly the same way. You'll find ways to help your group learn and think under pressure, much as the biology professor did in my story.

As you've seen, there's not a lot of specific technical knowledge in this book. As I see it, my job is to:

- Motivate you to develop your own version of an emergency medical aid program for kids.
- Inform you about the tools at your disposal—this book is one of those—and inspire you to use them. The Internet, reference books, and emergency medical specialists, trainers, and consultants can provide much more in the way of technical information.
- Convince you I'm right when I say, "Children would rather help in an emergency than be the cause of it."

# A Final Simulation

When I do a program, I like to cap it off with a simulation—a complex role-play dramatization that integrates all the material I've presented and is designed to be as realistic as possible. The students first choose a "victim" from their group. They then concoct a story to give the "rescuer" (played by me). After they apply the make-up and position the props, they send two group members to find me and ask for assistance.

This is fun for them. Since I'm the one on the spot, no one feels pressured to perform. They can see how one person can come into a scene after being sure it's safe, arrange for outside assistance, scan for life-threatening problems, keep anyone else from causing problems, and then give little c.p.r. to the injured person until outside help arrives.

Are you willing to place yourself in this same spot, with all your students scrutinizing your every word and move? Practice a few times beforehand on imaginary victims, always realizing that your group may "catch" you doing something that isn't what you wanted them to learn!

Bear in mind that the process of story creation, make-up application, and the actual simulation should be done fairly rapidly. It's also probably best to have only one victim. If you want to incorporate two or more, then part of the learning will be concerned with triage—determining who needs help the most.

### Simulation Ground Rules

- Designate just one victim.
- Victim must be conscious.
- Crying, sobbing, yelling, and screaming is permitted
- Victim may appear to be uncooperative.
- At least two people must go to the rescuer with information: what's wrong, how many people are involved, and what is being done for them.
- Observers (those not directly part of the simulation) should position themselves so they can see and hear all that happens when the rescuer interacts with the victim. I ask them to behave as if they were watching a play, except they will be asked questions after the simulation is completed.

Before preparing for the simulation, introduce your group to *moulage*, which is a fancy word for make-up used to simulate injuries. Show them what moulage material is available to them, how to use it, and how to clean up after the simulation is over. In *Teaching Aids* (p.146), I've listed some moulage items I use for quick and simple injury simulations.

## Questions & Answers

I find it useful to quiz students after the simulation has been completed. I've listed sample questions here, along with some of the answers I've received.

## Questions & Answers

**What did you see me do before I went over to the victim?**

You checked to see if it was safe to go to the victim.

**Before I touched the victim, what did I say and what did you see me doing?**

You found out the victim's name and gave her your name. Then you did a very quick overall survey, looking for any life-threatening problems.

**What did I do next?**

You told the victim help was on the way, assured her you'd keep others from causing more difficulties, and asked for more information about what had happened.

**Why did I cover her with that "space blanket" thing?**

To keep her warm and dry; to give her some privacy. (*The "space blanket thing" is also called a rescue blanket. I think one should be part of any emergency kit. Such blankets are light, inexpensive, and very useful.*)

**Did I do anything else?**

You talked to her, offered to hold her hand, and said you would do all you could to make her feel better. You gave her little c.p.r.

**Could you have done this yourself?**

Yes!

## Notes:

# Teaching Aids

ere are some of the gimmicks I've found useful, along with some suggestions on how to find props and make moulage on your own.

**Props: Where To Find Them, How To Make Them**
Props to make the role-play seem more realistic can make a big difference in learning these skills. You can find the basic supplies at your local drug store, supermarket, outdoor store, or party supply store. Here's how to make some of the basics.

**Blood**—Mix red food coloring with pancake syrup or honey until you like the result. Tastes pretty good, too! To make *lots* of blood (so that you can show your group what massive bleeding looks like, or to show them how much blood is taken when it's donated) use red water instead of syrup. Powdered drink mix (cherry Kool-Aid, for example), is an inexpensive way to make the water red.

A clear pint container (an empty water bottle, for example) makes a good prop to show kids how much blood is taken when someone donates blood at the Red Cross. Slowly pouring that out onto a tarp (see below) or piece of light-colored carpet (pick up a scrap from someone who sells it) dramatically shows that just a small amount of blood looks like a lot.

Warm water, food coloring, and a Camelbak or Platypus hydration pack can make a terrific simulated show of massive arterial bleeding when the bladder holding the "blood" is hidden in the "victim's" clothing and the mouth of the tube placed at the site of the "wound." You can buy the hydration system at a bike shop or outdoor store, or perhaps you know someone who has an old one they're willing to lend or donate.

To simulate blood drooling from the mouth, buy large, empty gelatin capsules from the drug store. Fill one of these with your "blood" mixture, then let the victim hold it in her mouth until the rescuer enters the scene. Then, have her bite down, drool, and cough.

*Pieces of facial tissue or eyeglass cleaning papers rubbed with cooking oil or petroleum jelly make sick-looking blisters, especially on the face.*

**Vomit**—Food coloring comes in little packages of several bottles containing different colors. Mix some colors with a small amount of water until it looks the way you want it to, then add raw oatmeal or crushed crackers. Stir in either tuna fish or sardines for a strong smell and mix it all together in a small container. Of course, with such a mess in your role-play victim's mouth, he may vomit anyway!

**Burns**—Pieces of facial tissue or eyeglass cleaning papers, rubbed with cooking oil or petroleum jelly, make sick-looking blisters, especially on the face. Washable felt markers can add extra realism—see description below under "Fake Body Parts and Wounds."

**Tears**—Glycerin, along with an eye dropper and small bottle (all available at your drug store), can make great fake tears. Be careful not to actually place glycerin drops in your victim's eyes. Put them alongside the nose, just below the eye.

**Real Bones and Other Tissue**—Great broken bones (complete with the sound and feel when you snap them) can be made from dried chicken or turkey leg bones. Someone in the meat department of your local supermarket should be able to help you with bigger bones. Thigh bones are especially useful for showing your group what happens when a bone breaks and the sharp ends are left to puncture blood vessels and stick into muscles.

Chances are, your butcher can furnish you with good examples of knee and elbow joints, too—cartilage and all. Turkey and chicken joints work as well. It's a good idea to soak the bones in a solution of bleach and water, then let them dry in the sun for several days before using. Be sure to keep them out of reach of your dog.

If your area has a slaughter house or a place where deer hunters take their kill to be processed, you have a treasure trove of bones and other structures to show your group. There's nothing like some actual brain matter or intestines to liven up a class!

*Great broken bones can be made from dried chicken or turkey leg bones. Thigh bones are especially useful for showing your group how jagged bone ends can damage surrounding tissue.*

**Fake Body Parts and Wounds**—Party stores that carry Halloween items are an excellent resource. The best selection is available before October 31, but best prices are found after that date. Fake blood, blisters, and tears come in very handy for simulations.

A simple trick is to use washable marking pens. Red ones are great for simulating a gash on a leg, face, or arm. Just add fake blood. Mixing colors (blue, black, red, yellow) can make a nasty-looking bruise, especially if you're using water-based pens. Permanent markers don't mix as well and stay on the skin for days after you wish they were gone.

You can also use theatrical paint from a party store or theatrical supply. You might prefer this over the marking pens, since it can be blended easily and is removable with tissues, cold cream, or hand cleaner (watch out for abrasive cleaners used by mechanics). Use white to indicate pallor and blue on the lips to simulate hypothermia. Red mixed with blue and black makes a nice purple bruise. Using too many colors is going to cause your victim to look as if he's had someone do face painting on him instead of like someone who's been hurt.

**Deep Lacerations**—For simulating lacerations, two items are useful. One is easy to find; the other gives a more realistic effect, but is harder to locate.

**1** Playdough or modeling clay
Warm the clay by rolling it in your hands (this is a great way to let your students help), then place it where you want the "cut." Use a warm, dull table knife (heat it in warm water), then shape the clay to suit your needs. Twisting the knife makes a more ragged-looking wound. Color with the washable markers, drip a little "blood" on them and—*yuk!*—there you have your laceration.

**2** Mortician's wax or Derma Wax
Harder to find is a soft, waxy material known as mortician's wax. The brand name to look for is Stein's

Derma Wax. It may be available from a funeral home or from a store that specializes in make-up for stage plays. You can embed splinters of wood, glass, or metal in this wax and create very realistic-looking puncture wounds. Take care not to push too hard on the embedded items or you may have a *real* wound on your hands!

**Compound or Open Fractures**—Obtain pieces of bone from a chicken carcass or from a butcher at the supermarket. Boil bones thoroughly to remove any flesh, then break into usable-sized pieces by placing them in a towel, rag, or sock and smashing with a hammer. Embed the bones in modeling clay, as described above. Add a bit of fake blood, and you're in business.

**Constructing a Stage**

Constructing a simple stage or venue for teaching is important. My favorite prop here is a waterproof nylon tarp. Not only does it provide a place for the group to gather while you are talking with them, it is also useful when staging a simulation. "Blood" or other liquids can be cleaned from the tarp easily, and if the simulation is happening outdoors, it keeps your make-believe victim off the ground.

For me, the perfect tarp is 10 ft. X 10 ft., and light in color, which makes it easier to see "blood." Find a cheap one at a thrift or discount store. If you can't find the right tarp, a large carpet remnant will also do the job.

**Other Resources**

Community colleges, universities, the Red Cross, fire department training officers, rescue squads, and police departments sometimes have equipment to lend you or staff to help you, or both. Take the time to explain to them what you're teaching. When they understand what you're trying to accomplish, they'll likely be more than willing to assist.

High school or college drama departments may also have students who create special effects for plays and who could help. People who do this sort of thing usually love to show others the results of their efforts.

Finally, you can go to the Internet and search for the words "moulage" and "casualty simulations " to find the type of materials that EMS, rescue, and emergency preparedness people use in their training simulations. You'll be surprised at what's out there. Expect to spend a lot of money if you go this route.

## Notes:

# The First Aid Kit

## The First Aid Kit in Your Head

Your best first aid kit is between your ears. The more you know and understand about injuries, the better you can deal with them. Learning to quickly recognize whether a problem is serious or not is a vital skill. Sometimes, injuries that look horrible are not that serious. Other times, injuries that can be deadly give only a few subtle clues.

For example, somebody who hits his head on a rock may get a cut to his skin. Even tiny cuts on the head can be very scary because they bleed a lot. Seeing someone with blood running down her face can seem like something right out of a horror film. It looks serious! But you know that if you just hold pressure on it for a while, you can control the bleeding.

Another time, someone may hit his head on a rock. It hurts for a minute and he gets a nice goose egg on his noggin, but he says he'll be fine. Twenty minutes later, he vomits. The first aid kit in your head tells you: head injury + vomiting = SERIOUS! This time the bleeding is on the INSIDE of his head. You know you need to get help for your friend fast.

### Keep Your First Aid Kit Well-Stocked

You have to keep the first aid kit in your head well-stocked and fresh. Learn all you can. Read about first aid, particularly related to your favorite activities. One good thing you can do is get a first aid certification that needs to be renewed. This way, every year or two you can get recertified and restock your mental first aid kit. Even if it's the same certification over and over again, different teachers will expand your knowledge through sharing their experiences and methods of teaching. Medical knowledge is always growing and changing.

### Make It *Your* First Aid Kit

There are many first aid kits available for sale. You can buy a small one in a grocery store or pharmacy. Maybe you'll get one as a gift. Regardless of the source, you need to make it *your* first aid kit. Open it up and take everything out of it. Inspect every item and learn what's there. Then figure out what's missing. For example, if you or someone in your group or family is allergic to bee stings, you may want to add an EpiPen (a pre-measured, injectable dose of epinephrine for anaphylactic shock) to your first aid kit.

Next, figure out what you don't need and exchange it for what you do need. Do you really think you'll need 20 gauze pads on this hike, or would it be better to exchange some of them for an elastic (Ace-type) bandage to treat a sprained ankle on the long walk?

### Make the Kit Fit the Activity

There's no perfect first aid kit. Unless we drive an ambulance everywhere we go, we'll never be able to carry all the equipment and supplies we need to address every single first aid situation. If your first aid kit is too large, you won't take it with you. Try to keep it as small as possible. One of the best ways to do this is to have several small first aid kits instead of one great big one. You won't want to carry that great big sack full of splints and bandages, bottles, ointments, and remedies if you're just going out for a day hike with a friend. You may not even want to carry a fanny pack for just an afternoon walk in the woods. But you can stuff an Ace bandage, a couple of Band-Aids, a few Tylenol, a small bottle of sunscreen, and a pen and paper in a pocket of your day pack and be prepared for at least the most likely injuries on your hike. On the other hand, if 6 friends are spending a week hiking through a wilderness area, you're going to want to be better supplied. Decide what goes in your first aid kit based on the situation.

*Recognize that many items have multiple uses. A few feet of duct tape wrapped around your water bottle can later be used to fasten a bandage, secure a splint, cover a hot spot to prevent a blister, and make Band-Aids.*

**Write This Down**

When we build a first aid kit, we think about bandages, medicines, splints, and tools to help us deal with minor injuries. But what can we do to prepare for major injuries? In serious medical situations our response is to get help. The most important first aid tool for a serious injury is a pen and paper. *Make sure your first aid kit has a pen and paper.* Write down the name of the injured person (if you know it) and the telephone number of who needs to be called (Mom, Dad, a friend). Write down what happened, when, where, and what you have done so far. If you've taken any vital signs like heart or breathing rate, include them—especially if you have two or three sets. This vital information will help rescuers get to the injured person faster and be better prepared to handle the emergency.

**Versatility Is the Key**

Finally, choose items that can do more than one job. One of those small Swiss Army knives with scissors and tweezers is a great tool to have in your kit. A large-bore needle (16 to 14 gauge) like they use in hospitals makes a great little probe for digging out splinters. Recognize that many items have multiple uses. Bee sting anesthetic not only numbs the area around a sting, it will also numb an area for digging out splinters or cleaning up a scrape. A few feet of duct tape wrapped around your water bottle can later be used to fasten a bandage, cover a hot spot to prevent a blister, and make Band-Aids. Sanitary napkins make great, cheap, sterile bandages.

Now that you've got your tools together to fit the situation, rely on the most important first aid kit you have—the one in your head—to use them effectively.

## Notes:

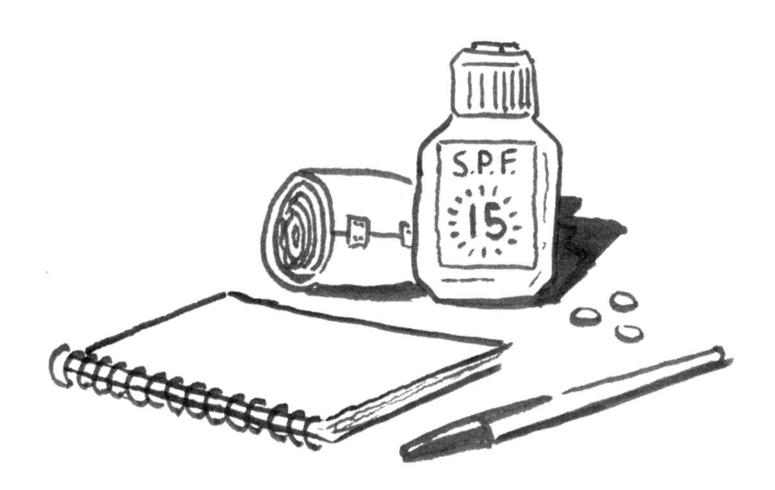

# Nuts & Bolts:
## Preparing Your WEMA Classes

A full WEMA class should run around 3 hours, max. Spreading it over 3 sessions of an hour each makes it less stressful for everyone. And make no mistake—teaching and learning this material *is* stressful. After all, you're constantly presenting and talking about what to do in life and death situations.

**Before You Begin**

Give yourself plenty of time to review this book thoroughly. You'll find some things that are important, others not so important. Use your triage skills to prioritize. Ask yourself, "If I had to do this WEMA in one hour, what would I teach and what would I leave out?" Or try a what-if: "What if these kids left my class today, then encountered a life-threatening situation before our next session. What would I want them to know?" The answer will be a distillation of what you consider to be the most critical sections of this book. Sure, it's *all* important, but depending on your group, some issues are more important than others.

Most of the WEMA courses I do have three sessions that last about an hour each. Here is one way to structure them.

**WEMA Session 1**

First, I have every participant fill out a name tag and put it on. I introduce myself and ask everyone else to do the same, giving their name and reason for being in the class. I give a quick explanation of how the class will be organized before I actually begin teaching.

- Start with a gory story—an attempt to draw the students in and show them how they could be heroes in life-threatening situations. Begin with one of the stories in this book, or use one from your own background.

- Emphasize personal safety at the outset, being sure students understand they must keep themselves safe if they are to be of help to the victim.
- Cover *Contacting 911* next. This fits in nicely when, in the story, the rescuer cannot enter the scene safely.
- After that, move to *The Big 3* immediately. Cover *Breathing*, then *Bleeding*, then *Bumped Heads*. These are problems that can't wait for 911 help to arrive at the scene.
- Introduce little c.p.r.
- Before ending Session 1, succinctly review with your group all the points you've covered. Remember that even though not everyone present may return for your second session, everyone will leave with important information.

Covering all of this at your first session will be a challenge. Aim for it because you may not see these children again, and you are giving them information that could save the life of someone they care about very much!

**WEMA Session 2**

- Begin this session with *Critter Problems*. Kids love to tell stories about their encounters with animals. Use their stories to emphasize important points in this material. This time, your students are the storytellers.
- Present the material in *Broken Bones*, *What About Burns?*, and *When Something's Just Not Right*. Do this in whatever order suits you. You may have time for even more material, so remember to over-prepare, just in case.

**WEMA Session 3**

- Present prevention. Use the story from *The Big P* chapter to begin this session. Not only is the story true, it illustrates a number of things that could have prevented the accident and injury.
- Your class finale will be a simulated emergency and a quiz afterward. (See *A Final Simulation* [p.142] for simulation guidelines.) This is where your group gets to use the moulage materials to make the simulation more realistic (See *Teaching Aids*, p.146), and you play the rescuer, demonstrating how to interact with a conscious victim. ("Conscious" means awake and alert, that is, the victim is "with you"—not in a drug-induced state, and able to communicate with you intelligently. Note that agitation and fear are both normal in an injured person.) Be sure to demonstrate little c.p.r. in this role.
- You may decide to have a question and answer wrap-up after the simulation. I like to do that at the very end of the last session.

**General Guidelines**

- When preparing for a simulation, It's a good idea for you to rehearse giving little c.p.r. before class, including (1) entering the scene, (2) introducing yourself to the victim, (3) securing permission to treat the victim, (4) doing a quick head-to-toe survey for serious injuries, (5) assuring the victim you're going to protect them from further injury while explaining your plans, (6) covering the victim (if possible) to prevent heat loss and provide a measure of privacy. Rehearsing can make a big difference in how your demonstration of these skills comes across to your group.
- Allow ample time for questions and answers. This time may be less structured, but it's a great way to sneak in additional material.

- In general, plan your time carefully, and err on the side of overpreparedness. There's nothing worse than running out of material long before the class period is over, or before parents come to collect their kids. So prepare way more material than you plan to cover in each session.
- Don't count on the "what-if" scenes to fill the time allotted for your students. Again, err on the side of overpreparedness. If you run out of time, you can always start the next session with any material you didn't get to in the last one. If the students are interested, they'll remember their questions from the previous class.

If you don't have time to cover everything here, be judicious about what you omit. By now I'm sure you've realized there's a lot of "meat" packed into WEMA—almost more than there is time to teach.

# A Body of Facts

These bits of fascinating information were discovered in the course of compiling the resources I recommend at the end of this book. Some of this information also came from web sites. A curious person could find much, much more by browsing in an encyclopedia or snooping around on the Internet.

**General Human Body**

1. The thickness of your skin varies from 0.02 in. at the eyelids to 0.24 in.at the soles of your feet.

2. You lose millions of skin cells each day. Over a year's time, you might lose as much as 5 lbs. of dead skin cells. Most household dust is made up of dead skin cells.

3. The hair on your head grows about 1/2 in. each month, lasts for 3 to 4 years, then falls out. Every day we lose 10 to100 strands of hair, but gain about the same number.

4. Fingernails grow about 0.02 in. each week, much faster than toenails.

5. When you sneeze, the air comes out of your nose at over 100 mph and can spray germs and mucus as far as 10 ft.

6. The body of a normal adult contains about 10 gallons of water, making up about 60 percent of the body weight.

7. If your normal body temperature was 86° F, you could live to be 200 years old.

8. There is enough phosphorus inside the human body to make about 250 matches.

9 A human egg is smaller than a pinhead.

10 Human skin is waterproofed by waxes, oils, and other protective substances it produces. Without them, you'd soak up bath water like a sponge.

**Circulatory System**

11 Each drop of human blood contains about 6 million blood cells. Each cell works for about 3 months, then is replaced. Iron and protein in discarded red blood cells are recycled in the bone marrow.

12 There are about 1,000 red blood cells for every white one. (That's why blood is red and not white.)

13 Actually, white blood cells have no color. Their job is to keep the blood healthy. When they've done their job, they sometimes appear as yellowish-white near the site of a wound, in the form of pus.

14 The body has about 60,000 miles of blood vessels. These vessels move blood all around your body.

15 With each squeeze of your heart, a little less than one third of a cup of blood is pumped out.

16 In one day, your heart moves almost 1,800 gallons of blood throughout your body.

17 A typical human heart beats approximately 3 billion times, starting about 6 months before birth.

18 A typical human heart is about the size of an average adult's fist and weighs about the same as 2 baseballs.

19 The average heart is strong enough to send a squirt of blood about 6 feet into the air.

20 It takes just 60 seconds for an adult heart to pump all of her blood (4 to 5 quarts) around her entire body.

**21** In one year, a child's heart beats about 47 million times, assuming the normal heart rate for a child— 80 to 100 beats per minute.

**22** The shrew, one of the smallest of all mammals, has a heart rate of around 1,000 beats per minute.

**23** An elephant's heart beats at 20 to 30 beats per minute.

**24** At rest, a highly trained bicycle racer's heart beats at around the same speed as that of an elephant.

**25** Capillaries are so small that 10 of them together would only be as thick as one human hair.

**26** White blood cells are twice as large as red cells.

**27** Your heart beats around 100,000 times each day without ever resting.

**28** A typical human heartbeat lasts about $^{8}/_{10}$ of a second.

**29** Teenagers have about a gallon of blood in their bodies; adults have a bit more.

**30** When you were born, your body had about 12 oz. ($^{3}/_{4}$ of a pint) of blood.

**31** Your liver is the largest organ in your body and weighs around five pounds.

**32** A human liver filters about 6 cups of blood per minute.

**33** If 90 percent of your liver was removed, the remaining 10 percent could regrow the whole organ.

**34** Every day, a pair of human kidneys filters about 44 gallons of liquid. Most of this is recycled, leaving less than half a gallon to be removed from the body by urination.

**35** One set of human blood vessels, put end to end, could go $2\,^{1}/_{2}$ times around the Earth at the equator.

**36** The longest vein in your body is the great saphenous vein, which extends from your foot to your pelvis.

**37** The largest blood vessel in your body is the aorta. Nearly 1 in. in diameter, it goes all the way from your breastbone to the hamstring muscles in the back of your leg.

**Respiratory System**

**38** Over a lifetime, you will inhale about 13 million cubic feet of air. That's enough to fill about 52 Goodyear blimps.

**39** On an average day, you will breathe about 24 ,000 times. In an average lifetime of 70+ years, that's more than 6 million breaths.

**40** At rest, a human being breathes about 14 times each minute.

**41** The surface area of your lungs is about 40 times greater than that of your skin.

**42** You have about 700 million alveoli in your lungs. From these tiny air sacs, oxygen passes into your blood and waste gases are taken out.

**Nervous System**

**43** The brain grows from 14 oz. at birth to about 46 oz. at adult size.

**44** Our sense of smell is about 10,000 times more sensitive than our sense of taste. Compared with that of other animals, our sense of smell is not all that great.

**45** Smell happens inside your nose. There are millions of chemoreceptors (smell receptors) inside your nose, but they only take up about as much room as a postage stamp.

**46** You never forget a smell, so you may be able to recognize thousands of smells.

47 When you have a cold, you often lose your sense of smell because the chemoreceptors are blocked by excess mucus.

48 The adult human brain weighs about 3 lbs. and uses about 20 percent of the body's blood and oxygen.

49 The brain is made up of around 100 billion neurons.

50 The brain receives over 100 million messages per second, from all over our bodies.

51 Nerves send messages to various parts of our bodies at about 250 mph.

52 You blink about 15,000 times each day.

53 In a single day, the lens in your eye may change shape 100,000 times.

54 The longest nerve in your body is the sciatic nerve, running from the lower end of the spinal cord downward into each leg. It is strong enough to suspend 400 lbs.

**Digestive System**

55 Your body creates almost 2 quarts of saliva a day.

56 The lining of your stomach has 35 million glands and produces 2 to 3 quarts of stomach juices per day.

57 From the time food goes into your mouth to when it leaves your body as waste, it has moved through about 30 ft. of "plumbing" in about 15 hours.

58 The average adult stomach processes about 1,100 lbs. of food each year.

59 Over a 70-year life span, even accounting for smaller meals during childhood, an American eats about 33 tons of food, roughly the weight of 6 elephants.

60 The large intestine is 5 ft. long, whereas the small intestine is 16 to 19 ft. long.

61 Urine is about 95 percent water and 5 percent waste.

62 When you swallow, peristaltic wave contractions push the food or drink along at 1 to 2 in. per second.

**Musculoskeletal System**

63 You have about 600 muscles in your body. (Try to sit absolutely still, so that no muscles are moving. Impossible!) Your heart beats at 70 to 80 pumps per minute, and your eyes blink about 15 times per minute.

64 The longest, heaviest, and strongest bone in your body is the femur (thighbone). Its length is usually about a quarter of your total height.

65 The smallest bone in your body is deep inside your ear and is called the stapes, which means stirrup. It measures about 1/4 in. long.

66 Your skull may feel like one solid bone, but it's actually made up of 28 separate bones interlocked like pieces of a jigsaw puzzle.

67 The only movable bone in your skull (not counting the three inside each of your ears) is your mandible or lower jaw bone.

68 Most people go to bed shorter than when they wake up in the morning. This is because the cartilage between each of our vertebrae becomes flattened by the weight of the body during the day.

69 Your "funny bone" is not a bone. It's actually the ulnar nerve that runs through your elbow and tingles when bumped hard.

**70** Did anyone ever tell you it takes more muscles to frown than to smile? It takes at least 14 different muscles to smile. An estimated 43 muscles are used when you frown.

**71** The muscles in your body make up nearly half your total weight.

**72** Humans can make over 7,000 facial movements.

**73** When you clamp down on your molars, your jaws can generate about 200 lbs. of force.

**74** The most frequently broken human bone is the clavicle (collarbone) because when you fall on your shoulder or arm, it's the bone that takes the force.

**75** The longest muscle in the human body is the sartorius, anchored at the hipbone and extending to the top of the tibia (shin bone).

**76** The smallest muscle in your body is the stapedius muscle. It pulls on the smallest bone in your body, the stapes, to protect your ear from loud noises.

**77** The largest muscle is the latissimus dorsi, the flat muscle of the back that operates during arm movement.

Here are the "accidents waiting to happen" I saw in the pictures on pages 82-85.

**Campsite**

- Broken glass on ground
- Fire built under tree
- Fuel too close to camp stove
- Axe blade exposed and left on ground
- Tent under hornet nest

**Kitchen**

- Stove burner left on
- Drawer open
- Poison under sink
- Puddle of water on floor
- Dishwasher left open
- Overloaded electrical socket

So, did I miss anything? Did you?

# Suggested Reading

## BOOKS FOR KIDS

*A Child's First Library of Learning: Our Bodies,* Time-Life Books, Alexandria, Va. 1988.

Avison, B., *I Wonder Why I Blink*, Kingfisher Books, New York 1993.

Brunn, R.A., and Beres, S., *101 Things Every Kid Should Know About the Human Body*, Lowell House, Los Angeles 1999.

Boelts, M. and D., *Kids To The Rescue: First Aid Techniques for Kids*, Parenting Press, Inc., Seattle, Wa. 1992.

Brunn, B., *The Human Body*, Random House, New York 1982.

*Buscaglia, L., *The Fall of Freddie the Leaf, A Story of Life For All Ages*, Holt, New York 1982.

*Darden, H.D., *The Everlasting Snowman,* Sunflower Publishing Co., Statesville, N.C. 1996.

*The Human Body*, Dorling Kindersley, London 1995.

*Munday, M., *Sad Isn't Bad: A Good-Grief Guidebook for Kids Dealing with Loss,* Abbey Press, St. Meinrad, Ind. 1998.

Parker, S., *The Body Atlas,* Dorling Kindersley, New York 1993.

*Especially helpful in grief counseling.

National Geographic Society, *Your Wonderful Body,* Washington, D.C., 1982.

Time-Life Student Library, *Human Body,* Alexandria, Va. 1999.

Tilton, B., *First Aid for Youths,* ICS Books, Merrillville, Ind. 1994.

VanCleave, J., *The Human Body for Every Kid,* John Wiley and Sons, New York 1995.

Whitefeather, W., *Outdoor Survival Book for Kids,* Harbinger House, New York 1990.

*Winch, J. L., *After the Funeral,* Paulist Press, New York 1995.

## BOOKS FOR TEACHERS

Auerbach, P., *Medicine for the Outdoors,* Lyons Press, New York 1999.

*Brooks, B. and Siegel, P., *The Scared Child,* John Wiley & Sons, New York 1996.

**35 Ways to Help a Grieving Child,* Dougy Center, Portland, Ore. 1999.

*Everything You Need to Know About Medical Emergencies,* Springhouse Corporation, Springhouse, Pa. 1997.

Forgey, W., *Wilderness Medicine: Beyond First Aid,* 5th Ed., Globe Pequot Press, Guilford, Conn. 2000.

Gill, P., *Pocket Guide to Wilderness Medicine & First Aid,* Ragged Mountain Press, Camden, Me. 1997.

Goold, G., and Vahradian, S., Basic First Response, Prentice-Hall, Upper Saddle River, N.J. 1997.

*Johnson, K., Trauma in the Lives of Children, Hunter House, Alameda, Ca. 1989.

*Kroen, W., *Helping Children Cope with the Loss of a Loved One*, Free Spirit Publishing, Inc., Minneapolis, Minn. 1996

*Kubler-Ross, E., *Questions and Answers on Death and Dying,* Macmillan, New York 1974.

*Nuland, S. B., *How We Die: Reflections on Life's Final Chapter,* Knoph, New York 1994.

Paton, B. (et al.), *Wilderness First Aid: Emergency Care for Remote Locations,* Jones and Bartlett Publishers, Sudbury, Me. 1998.

Preston, G., *Wilderness First Aid: When You Can't Call 911,* Falcon Publishing, Inc., Helena, Mont. 1997.

Rosenberg, S., and Dougherty, K., *The Complete Idiot's Guide to First Aid Basics,* Alpha Books, New York 1996.

Tilton, B., *The Wilderness First Responder,* Globe Pequot Press, Old Saybrook, Conn. 1998.

Wilkerson, J., *Medicine For Mountaineering & Other Outdoor Activities* (5th ed.), The Mountaineers, Seattle, Wash. 2001

*Wolfelt, A., *A Child's View of Grief,* Center for Loss and Life Transition, Fort Collins, Colo. 1991.

# About the Author

**Steve Longenecker** has been a teacher of one kind or another all of his adult life. He has been a junior high school teacher, a Red Cross First Aid and CPR Instructor Trainer, and a Wilderness First Responder. As a rock climber, he is credited with a number of classic first ascents in western North Carolina. He helped develop the outdoor programs for many summer camps in the region and currently serves as Adventure Programs Director at Falling Creek Camp for Boys.

Permitted by the U.S. Fish & Wildlife Service to use non-releasable birds of prey in educational programs, he has introduced thousands of children to the natural world of snakes and raptors through his presentations to school, Scout, church, and other youth groups.

Steve began teaching Wilderness Emergency Medical Aid for Kids in 1973. He continues to develop and provide programs for children and is available for WEMA classes as well as training workshops for adult leaders.

For more information, contact Steve at sfl@ioa.com or write him care of:

Falling Creek Camp
PO Box 98
Tuxedo, NC 28784
828-692-0262

# Milestone Press

## Outdoor Adventure Guides

**MOTORCYCLE ADVENTURE SERIES**
by Hawk Hagebak

- Motorcycle Adventures in the Southern Appalachians—
  North GA, East TN, Western NC
- Motorcycle Adventures in the Southern Appalachians—
  Asheville NC, Blue Ridge Parkway, NC High Country
- Motorcycle Adventures in the Central Appalachians—
  Virginia's Blue Ridge, Shenandoah Valley, West Virginia Highlands

**FAMILY ADVENTURE**
by Mary Ellen Hammond
& Jim Parham

- Natural Adventures in the Mountains of North Georgia

**OFF THE BEATEN TRACK MOUNTAIN BIKE GUIDE SERIES**
by Jim Parham

- Vol. I: Western NC—The Smokies
- Vol. II: Western NC—Pisgah
- Vol. III: North Georgia
- Vol. IV: East Tennessee
- Vol. V: Northern Virginia

- Tsali Mountain Bike Trails Map
- Bull Mountain Bike Trails Map

**PLAYBOATING**
by Kelly Fischer

- A Playboater's Guide to the Ocoee River
- Playboating the Nantahala River—An Entry Level Guide

# Milestone Press
## Outdoor Adventure Guides

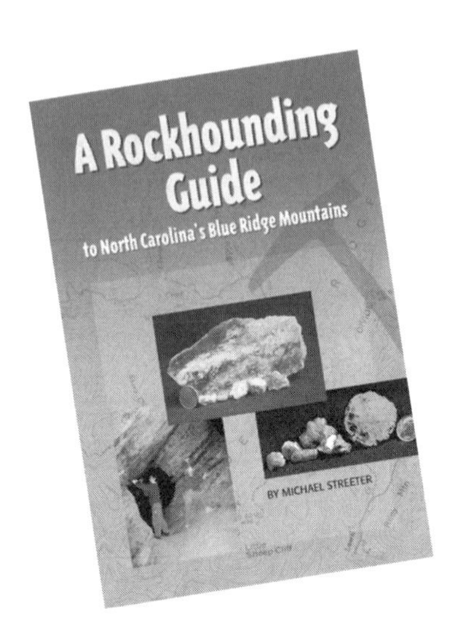

**ROCKHOUNDING**
by Michael Streeter

- A Rockhounding Guide to North Carolina's Blue Ridge Mountains

**ROAD BIKE SERIES**

- Road Bike Asheville, NC: Favorite Rides of the Blue Ridge Bicycle Club by The Blue Ridge Bicycle Club
- Road Bike the Smokies: 16 Great Rides in North Carolina's Great Smoky Mountains by Jim Parham
- Road Bike North Georgia: 25 Great Rides in the Mountains and Valleys of North Georgia by Jim Parham

## OUTDOOR EDUCATION

- Steve Longenecker's Wilderness Emergency Aid Book for Kids (& Their Adults)